GITA P

GITA FOR EVERYONE

AN ENGLISH TRANSLATION
WITH AN INTRODUCTION AND NOTES

BY
JOGINDRANATH MUKHARJI, BA

EDITED BY
SHANTANU MUKHARJI

RUPA

Published by
Rupa Publications India Pvt. Ltd 2000
7/16, Ansari Road, Daryaganj
New Delhi 110002

Sales centres:
Allahabad Bengaluru Chennai
Hyderabad Jaipur Kathmandu
Kolkata Mumbai

Edition Copyright © Shantanu Mukharji 2000

ISBN: 978-81-716-7489-3

Twelfth impression 2017

15 14 13 12

Typeset by Tarun Enterprise, Delhi

Printed at Shree Maitrey Printech Pvt. Ltd, Noida

ABOUT THE AUTHOR

About the Author

Jogindranath Mukharji (1871-1930) was born in Hooghly, Bengal. His father, Kapali Prasanna Mukharji, was the first Indian MA in English from Calcutta University. Kapali was a lawyer turned

ABOUT THE AUTHOR

Administration, and a scholar of Hindu sacred texts. Jogindranath graduated from Ripon College, Calcutta, in 1895. He migrated to the United Provinces (now Uttar Pradesh) around the turn of the century. He was Headmaster of several schools during his career. His most significant contribution, however, was as Principal of SM College, Chandausi (Moradabad), where he held the post from 1908 till his death in 1930.

The first edition of *Gita for Everyone* was published in 1900 under the title *Young Men's Gita*. Principal Mukharji was honoured with the title of 'Rai saheb' in 1926, for his dedication to the cause of education.

Dedication

I dedicate this book to the memory of my late grandfather Shri Jogindranath Mukharji. He was a noble and learned man who I was not destined to meet. I was unable to benefit from his wisdom except in the form of this book. My thanks are due to my father, Shri Shailendra Nath Mukharji, and my late uncle, Shri Girijapati Mukharji, who safeguarded the book himself before passing on this prized possession to me.

I wish to express my gratitude to my old friends and well-wishers, Kaminee and Rajen Mehra for inspiring me to attempt the second edition of this great epic. Bringing out this masterpiece would not have been possible without

DEDICATION

the efforts of my daughter, Anamika,
who burnt midnight oil going through
the text again and again before it finally
reached the stands.

— **Shantanu Mukharji**

CONTENTS

CONTENTS

PREFACE TO THE FIRST EDITION

This translation is meant to be read by anyone interested in acquainting themselves with the Gita. To make the reading simpler, an Introduction and some Notes have been added to the translated text.

The object of the Introduction is to explain briefly, from a Hindu point of view, the main doctrines of the Gita. Unsympathetic critics, in forming estimates of its worth, are often influenced by their own decided opinions on certain topics of popular Indian creeds or on the doctrines of the well-known schools of Hindu Philosophy, and thus generally fail to recognize its uncommon merit. It is complete in itself, and references to other systems of thought, developed on different principles, are apt to be more embarrassing than useful at the beginning.

The Gita is a book of rare excellence which ought to be read by every Indian and will amply repay perusal. A single reading may not create sufficient interest in it, nor even ensure a tolerable grasp of its main outlines; but, as it is a small book, two or three successive readings can be easily managed, and they will, no doubt, make a good impression.

Much benefit will be derived by frequently consulting the Sanskrit text, of which a copy may be easily procured at a nominal cost. Certain words and expressions in the original as well as their inadequate English equivalents are not properly understood unless their different uses in different parts of the text are carefully noted. References by chapter and verse given in the Notes at the end of the book may, it is hoped, offer some help in this respect.

CALCUTTA, OCTOBER, 1899

Preface to the Second Edition

The Gita, as the sacred book of the Hindus, has passed on its wisdom from generation to generation. This particular version of the Gita, no less sacred to our family, has also been with us for four generations now. A matter of family pride, it has been talked, rather, boasted about, ever since we can remember. Occasionally, it is brought out with reverence from its place of repose and the pages are turned, the importance of the book and the brittle leaves demanding, and receiving, due care and gentleness.

For its believers, the worth of the Gita perseveres, undimmed in its relevance to their daily lives. As a guide to their existence, its value lies not in the language it is written in, but in its content. Therefore this Gita in English only reaches out to a slightly different group of people, while its essence remains unchanged.

They say charity begins at home. Well, our family has been fortunate to read this simplified Gita all these years. Now we feel its time to share this book with so many in the larger world, who may benefit from it. After all, 'Vasudhaiva Kutumbakam', the world is my family.

—Shantanu Mukharji
New Delhi,
September 2000

INTRODUCTION.

SHRIMAD BHAGAVAD GITA is a well known book of very high authority among all classes of Hindus. It is now found as an episode in the Mahabharata, and comprises chapters XXV to XLII in the Bhishma Parva; but many consider it as an interpolation, and its authorship is thus in dispute. There is, however, no dispute as to its being the best and most authoritative exposition of Shri Krishna's religious and moral doctrines.

Age of the Gita.—The age is still unsettled. At the end of each chapter the book is described as an Upanishad and Yoga Shastra, but it is not held to be as old as some of the well known Upanishads. It mentions most of the Vedic gods, but none of the additional ones of the Puranas, not even the distinguished names of Narayana and Shiva. Of the reputed founders of the six Schools of Hindu Philosophy, only two are named, *viz.* Kapila and Vyasa,—the former as the highest *siddha* and the latter as the highest *muni.* Both *Prakriti* of the Sankhya Philosophy and *Maya* of the Vedanta are used, but often as synonyms, while the word *Yoga,* by which Patanjali's Philosophy is distinguished, is the most important in the book. Chap. II. 42-46 seem to allude to a doctrine not unlike Jaimini's. Thus when the Gita was composed the chief philosophical doctrines had already been known, though perhaps the standard treatises with their existing systematic arrangements were later productions. The synopsis called *Tattwa-samása* and attributed to Kapila, the *A'di Vidwan* or first philosopher, had, however, apparently been already in use with teachers and lecturers in imparting oral instructions; for, the adoption in the Gita of almost the same special terms could not be purely accidental.

Opinions as to the age of the Gita have been hazarded upon considerations of its doctrinal agreement or difference with the Vedas, its style and versification, its mode of treating the different subjects, etc.; but the opinions are so divergent as to fix the age between a century or two before, and a century or two after, the commencement of the Christian era.

Doctrine.—The *religious* doctrine is one of monotheism fed by moral activity, rational thought and pious devotion. The Supreme Brahma is held to have a twofold Prakriti (nature, power or energy), which manifests itself in the creation of unchangeable or immortal creature-souls and the ever-moving or changeable Force or Matter that evolves the Universe through certain stages (VII. 4, 5; VIII. 3, 4; XIII. 6). This Prakriti, however, does not represent the entirety of the Divine Nature and the Universe is thus a partial manifestation of the Divine Power (X. 42, XI. 37, XIII. 12). The Supreme Brahma is the source of immortal life, eternal virtue and unmixed bliss (XIV. 27); and the highest aim of every human being is best attained by self-adjustments in conformance to the highest human model of the age, whose godlike character and nature entitle him to be treated as God's representative (IX. 30-32).

The *practical* doctrine recognises activity to be lawful only for the sake of sacrifice (*Yajna*), in deference, apparently, to the ruling idea of the time, without reference to which it was not then possible to explain or develop the idea of *duty*. *Yajna* literally means *worship,* but the peculiar form it had assumed was one associated with the feeding, with sacrificial offerings, of Fire, as the first of the Vedic gods and their representative. These gods being subordinated to the Lord of Sacrifice, Vishnu, *Yajna* became the emblematic worship of that one Lord. The idea of *Yajna* seems to have gradually extended in scope. Every energy or impulse of man being a gift of the Lord, its due exercise, as an act of obedience to him, was held to be a sacrificial offering feeding the vital flame of the individual and society (IV. 23-33). Acts performed in this spirit constituted *Yajna* which, alone, was thus to be the motive of every action. The Gita improves upon this idea by enjoining renunciation of selfish aims and thus brings out prominently the idea of Right or Duty in connexion with religious piety. Even so serious an affair as war, undertaken as a duty in the above sense, becomes justifiable though it involves the slaughter of one's own dearest relatives and friends, or of a whole race or nation. Considerations of duty or right are therefore declared to be paramount over every other consideration. But duty implies a twofold effort, *viz.* the performance of what is right and the abstention from what is wrong. The former is called *Karma-Yoga* or, simply, *Yoga;* and the latter *Karma-Sannyasa* or simply *Sannyasa.* Both *Yoga* and *Sannyasa* are thus influenced by what is called the *Yoga-understanding,* or moral sense, which, in comparison with the *outer act,* is held to be superior (II. 49), to justify the outer act whether good or bad in effect (II. 51), and to secure mental peace and a disposition for service of God and man in thought, feeling and action (VI. 29-32).

These are the main doctrines of the Gita upon a plain rational construction of the text without importing special ideas from any other system or systems of thought. But learned commentators differing widely in opinion on vital questions of 'speculative' or 'practical' philosophy were anxious to obtain for their respective pet theories the support of the Gita which as a holy book was held in the highest veneration throughout India; and the result was that, each interpreting the text to suit his purpose, important passages received many interpretations, often inconsistent with one another. The mischief did not end here. So long the original commentators interpreted the text in consistent plans, upon definite lines of thought, but they were followed by a class of annotators who, apparently holding no definite opinions of their own, freely adopted a sort of eclecticism, construing one passage according to Shankaracharya, another according to Ramanuja, a third according to another, and so on. Thus the commentators and, especially, the later annotators, while acknowledging the unquestionable authority of the Gita, contributed to the formation of a mass of inconsistencies, which are now the most powerful weapons in the hands of hostile critics, not bound by its authority. The multiplicity of interpretations gives them a large scope for selection, and each, according to his own plan of warfare, finds ample opportunities of making use of such as can offer the least resistance to an intelligent attack.

The Christian Literature Society for India, some years ago, issued an edition of *The Bhagavad Gita : with an English translation, explanatory notes and an Examination of its doctrines,* the title-page containing a summary of the examiner's views in the following words :—

"It is shown that the Poem, while it contains some noble sentiments, teaches Polytheism and Pantheism; that God and the soul are one; that Rajas and Tamas proceed from God as well as Sattwa; that caste is a divine institution; while its Yoga doctrine is proved to be a delusion."

A Hindu, after carefully studying the Gita, will find difficulty in concurring with the examiner, and be disposed to attribute most of his views to misapprehension. In discussing them, however, it will be convenient to refer to his "Examination" which sets out his grounds in detail, and to deal with them in the order he has adopted in it.

"1. ARJUNA´ MORE HUMANE THAN KRISHNA."

After referring to Arjuna's expressions of grief (I 28-46) and Krishna's (II. 23), the examiner says, "Krishna does not seem the least sorry that Arjuna should have grieved at slaying his dearest relatives and friends, and calls the feeling 'base faint-heartedness.' Which feeling was the more humane? the more godlike?"

Without quarrelling over the use of the stinging epithet *base* in the translation, it would be desirable to consider the real point. Krishna deprecates the humane feeling as being *unsuited* to the occasion. When at the commencement of a *just* war and on the field of battle the most reliable general becomes overwhelmed with personal feelings like those of Arjuna, would it not be right for the general's friend to address him in the way Krishna addressed Arjuna? If a Wellington or a Washington were prepared to give up leadership on similar grounds on the field of battle, the question would not be whether his feeling was *humane,* but whether it was *right.*

"2. KRISHNA'S REASONING WITH ARJUNA."

The examiner says :—

"When Arjuna asked Krishna to tell him the right course of conduct, he received the reply given in II. 11-52. Three reasons are assigned why he should fight:

(1) The soul, unborn, everlasting, kills not, it is not killed. Weapons cleave it not, nor does the fire burn it. As a man casting off old garments takes others, so the soul casting off old bodies enters others that are new.

(2) A lawful battle was the highest duty of a Kshatriya, and death when fighting was an open

door to heaven.

(3) Looking alike on pleasure and pain, he would not incur sin.

The 2nd and 3rd reasons will be considered afterwards. Bishop Caldwell shows the fallacy of the first reason by supposing it acted upon in common life."

Then follows an extract partially reproduced below, which argues the point thus :—

"A man accused of murder neither denies his guilt, nor pleads that he committed the act in self-defence, but addresses the Court in the language of Krishna. 'It is needless,' he says, 'to trouble yourselves about the inquiry any further. The soul can neither kill, nor be killed. It is eternal and indestructible. When driven from one body it passes into another. Death is inevitable, and another birth is equally inevitable. It is not the part therefore of wise men, like the judges of this Court, to trouble themselves about such things.' Would the judges regard the defence as conclusive?

Certainly not.' & c."

It is clear the reasoning of Gita is misunderstood. Suppose the judges in the above extract in answer say: "Friend, your argument is not conclusive. Your soul is immortal, indeed, but it is not free from susceptibilities to pleasure and pain. We have taken all this into account, and for your sake as well as for that of society, we cut off your career of iniquity and crime, rid you of the heavy momentum of sin which is impelling you downward, and help you on to other life where you will have a better opportunity of purifying your tainted nature. If our sentence had the effect of killing you, body and soul altogether, we should feel great hesitation in approving a capital punishment in your case or in any case. It is no less for the welfare of your immortal soul than for that of society that we are going to kill your body, which cannot last forever."

Be it remembered that immortality and transmigration of the soul are put forward in support of a *right,* and *not* set up in defence of *wrong*; and that they have not the same bearing on the latter that they have on the former. Morality starts with the intuitive belief in the soul's unity and immortality, and in the Gita begins its teachings with the first axioms like Euclid, they cannot harm the moralist any more than Euclid's axioms can harm the developed mathematician.

The extract referred to goes on to point out how an adulterer or a thief may make a defence upon the assumptions of the Gita but the arguments are no better than the those of the hypothetical case of the murderer.

(TITLE) "3 THE TRUTH OF POLYTHEISM ACKNOWLEDGED"

This charge is founded on III. 11, 12; IV. 12; VII. 23; IX. 20, 21, 25. It is not clear whether by *polytheism* is implied a co-ordination of gods, or a sort of celestial hierarchy. The Gita nowhere assigns to these gods the position and power of the Supreme One. They are, at most, subordinate ministers, to carry out Divine behests. IX. 23 says that devout sacrifice with faith to *other gods* is really sacrifice to Bhagavan, but it is irregular, because, as explained in IX. 24, "I am the Lord of sacrifice," or, in other words, because the sacrificer's faith is irrational and therefore defective from ignorance which can secure him no permanent good.

Belief in gods, angels, evil spirits, etc., was common in early ages, when the imagination supplied the place of scientific observation. Such belief is not easily shaken when there is no means of proving that spiritual beings of different grades and characters do not or cannot exist.

Krishna lived in an age when Pitris, etc. were held to be real beings, belief in whose existence it was then impossible shake, in the absence of those scientific rules of proof which are now adopted in methods of investigation. He did the best it was possible for him to do. He *assumed* the existence of gods, Pitris, etc., for argument's sake, and, pointing out their imperfections, in fact, nullified them.

"4. PANTHEISM TAUGHT."

References are made to VII. 4, 5, 6, 10 and 20, 22, 23, 29, 39 to support the above.

Now by VII. 4, 5, 6, the Lord declares to effect : "I have a *Prakriti* (power or energy) which manifests itself in the subtle elements and the thought-medium, and I have another *Prakriti* which manifests itself in the creature-soul. These two *Prakritis* supply constituent materials of all creatures, while I (*i.e.* by My Will) create and dissolve the Universe." In other words, He says "I have both *Power* and *Will* to create." The Christian doctrine holds that the Divine Will created the Universe *out of nothing,* but the Divine Will really includes the Divine Power (the Prakriti of Gita), and thus the expression *out of nothing* implies no essential difference between the doctrine of the Gita and the Christian doctrine. V. 10 uses the word *seed* in the sense of *cause* and does not seem to countenance pantheism. X. 20, 22, etc., in fact, all the verses 20-40, describe the Lord as being such and such things, acts or conditions. Do the verses mean to declare His identity with them, or to declare Him as the First Cause? That they do not mean the former alternative is evident from verses 41 and 42, especially the last half of v. 42. Besides, IX. 4, 5 and 6 expressly declare that creatures are distinct from God, and X. 20-40 should be consistently interpreted. Certain forms of loose expressions are common. As, for example, in pointing out a book on Geometry I may say, "This book is Euclid," and yet I do not mean that the book is the man Euclid. I simply mean that it, or rather its content, is the production of Euclid who, bodily, is no longer in the land of the living. It is in this sense than X. 20-40 are to be interpreted, *viz.*, that God is the Ultimate Cause of all that exists, and that each and all should be viewed in relation to Him in order to understand Him. When a devout man sees God in every leaf or in every flower, he simply realizes God's power and design. Apart from IX. 4, 5 and 6 and X. 41 and 42, the general tenor of the Gita which so prominently inculcates personal duties is against the Pantheistic doctrine. From a rationalistic point of view, it will be impossible to deny that the Universe is but a perceptible expansion of the potent Will of God.

II. 61, V. 29, VI. 31, VIII. 22, IX. 34, X. 10, 11, XI. 55, XII. 1-20, XIII. 12-17, XIV. 26, 27, XV. 17, and XVIII. 65, 66 leave no room for *pantheism*, either in the sense that, "God and nothing else exists," or in the sense that, all things are His parts and constitute His totality. The theory of the Gita is that God's power makes and unmakes the Universe at His will, but that this power or this will, which is limited to the Universe, is not the entirety of the Divine Nature.

"5. KRISHNA'S INCARNATIONS."

It may be stated at the outset that the Hindu theory of incarnation recognises the necessity of successive incarnations, from time to time, by example to re-invigorate virtue in her eternal struggle with vice. The incarnation of the age is thus the model man or God-man of that age, the cause and object of whose mission are declared in IV. 6-8. Does Krishna fulfil the ideal of his time? or of the present age? The answer to this question is not the same from all Hindu sects. The followers of Chaitanya hold him to have superseded Krishna. Krishna has been portrayed variously, and even among Vaishnavas, no two sects adopt the same model. We are concerned with the Krishna of the Gita, not every false Krishna that a Sanskrit versifier may choose to construct out of his imagination. The Puranik writers are responsible for the manner in which his life has been narrated. His sports in boyhood have been described as those of a young lover of women. It is often asked, if he was born to raise and sustain virtue, how was it that he countenanced polygamy? Hostile critics are, however, good enough to admit that there is much exaggeration regarding the number of his wives. To assign a she-bear for one of the eight principal wives is the height of absurdity. Many Hindus commending the ingenuity of the writers see the eight *Sankhya Prakritis* in the 8 principal wives and the 16 *Sankhya vikaras* or modifications (each manifesting in a thousand or numberless ways) in the 16,000 new wives. Divesting the narrations of allegorical elements and suggestions we must perhaps have still to assume that Krishna was a polygamist. *Absolutely* monogamy or polygamy is neither good nor bad, its goodness or badness depends upon circumstances. Even now an enlightened State has felt the expediency of recognising polygamy, in disregard of all past traditions of its own and examples in other states and countries. It is confessed that narrators of the life and doings of Krishna are not always felicitous in their performances, but they yet supply materials for an estimate of his character and dispositions, his unselfishness, his loving and amiable nature, his readiness and zeal in the cause of individual or public good, his learning and his practical sagacity. The Krishna of the Gita is, at least, irreproachable, and on the face of the excellent teachings it contains, one sees no just ground for hunting up matters from apocryphal stories and legends to lower the ideal.

"6. CREATION."

On this point the reader is referred to the remarks under "PANTHEISM TAUGHT." Theories about creation, Divine nature and attributes, and similar topics are all based upon Revelation or sayings of great men held to have been inspired. If, as some think, these inspirations were due to the workings of their individual imaginations, then all theories must be attributed to human imagination with some admixture of human reason which avoids glaring absurdities. The utility of quarrelling over hypotheses which can be neither proved nor disproved is not very apparent. They are, at best, happy hypotheses and no more. It is impossible to say how much of the present condition of Hindu society is attributable to them. Mere co-existence of two things does not imply the relation of cause and effect; for then one may be right in attributing drunkenness being found to prevail among men who dress themselves in that fashion.

Prejudice and error everywhere owe their continuance to the absence of scientific knowledge and scientific research. But in this cause the men of religion have seldom been zealous. Indeed, so long as scientists and philosophers were in a minority, the men of religion were the inveterate enemies of science and scientists, exerting all their social and political influence to check their progress. Now that scientific knowledge and scientific discoveries and inventions have remarkably helped the cause of human improvement and welfare, they are claimed as the legitimate results of the purity of a particular form of religion. The fact is that the priesthood of every country were the first to think on any subject and acquire the first few rudiments of general knowledge, but after obtaining a social influence had no incentive for fresh research, if by repressing the spirit of enquiry, whenever it arose among the lay public, they could maintain their superiority. The progress and development of science and correct thought are hardly attributable to the priesthood of any country. It is the natural disposition to activity and the spirit of enquiry to which all this progress is due.

The deteriorated Hindu is the product of many causes, of which not the least important is the accumulated influence on many generations of an enervating climate and the abundance of food supply fostering general indolence, an active imagination, a spirit of contentment, consequent disinclination for physical and mental efforts, attachment to stereotyped institutions, readiness to accept every absurdity as knowledge if it does not interfere with existing institutions, etc. The Hindu has enough of religious dogmas and moral maxims not less refined than any possessed by the most enlightened peoples of the world. What he wants is love of activity, which should be developed and sustained by a succession of worthy aims and motives.

"7. THE THREE 'GUNAS' PROCEED FROM KRISHNA."

Referring to VII. 12 and III. 36 the examiner says :—

"Passion and darkness proceed from God as well as goodness. A man is, as it were, by force compelled to commit sin. Hence man is not a free agent. We blame the thief and murderer, and hold them responsible for their actions, but if the Bhagavad Gita is true, we should blame no man, for he is compelled by Krishna to do this. Indeed, we ought to praise the greatest criminal, for he is only fulfilling the will of God. What a blasphemous doctrine is this !

"The Christian Scriptures, on the other hand, declare that 'God is light; and in Him is no darkness at all.' God is spotlessly pure, and no evil desire can arise in Him or from Him."

We would assume the examiner makes no intentional misinterpretation. We therefore translate VII. 12 as literally as possible :—

Those whose natures are *good,* and those who are *passionate* or *dark,* are indeed from Me (*i.e.,* created by Me). Understand them to be so, but not that I am in them (or) they are in Me. vii. 12.

What is wrong in the above

proposition? Is it denied that God created the angels, the men, the beasts, in fact, all creatures, rational, irrational, good, bad and indifferent? Is there anything which is supposed to affect the holiness of God who is "the Light of lights and said to be beyond darkness"? (XIII. 17).

Then as to the argument founded on III. 36, which in fact is a question by Arjuna. Let it be, however, assumed that the Lord is also of the opinion that man is, as it were, impelled to commit sin. The examiner overlooks the expression "as it were" and jumps to the conclusion "Hence man is not a free agent." If man were not held to be a free agent, what would be the utility of the precepts in vers. 41 and 42? Ver. 37 says that *desire* is the cause of sin and *the enemy* in the world. Substitute the Hebrew word *Satan* for *enemy* and a Christian will readily appreciate the force of the passage. Satan, created in heaven, became the archfiend and was allowed by God to prowl about in quest of prey, to tempt men to commit sin. He sought and obtained God's *express* permission to try Job. He was even allowed to tempt Jesus for 40 days in the wilderness. These are, of course, not historical facts, but the report of the 40 days' temptation could only originate from Jesus himself and at any rate no Christian can be disposed to deny its truth. In the opinion of Jesus, God often tempts or abets tempting; for his model prayer contains the significant words "lead us not into temptation" and seems to point out to God the motive for such abstention in the words "For Thine is the kingdom, and the power, and the glory, for ever."

III. 36 and VII. 12 are evidently misunderstood.

"8. KRISHNA ALIKE TO ALL, WITH ITS CONTRADICTION."

The examiner quotes IX. 29 (first half), and XVI. 19, 20 with Mr. Telang's remark "these persons (demoniac people) are scarcely characterised with accuracy as neither hateful nor dear to Krishna."

Now, IX. 29 runs thus :—

"Alike am I to all creatures. None is hateful or dear to Me. But they who serve Me with devoutness, they are in Me and I too am in them."

The whole verse clearly shows that by *alike* is meant *impartial* or *evenly just*. A minister of justice, say, a Sessions Judge, during the trial of a case in which are arrayed on both sides distinguished counsel, says: "I am alike to both parties. I love or hate neither. Whichever of you serves the cause of justice, he and I are one." If "alike" means "impartial" or "just" XVI. 19 and 20 are not in conflict with IX. 29, or with Divine Justice.

Other contradictions referred to are the following :—

"In Book xii. 12, concentration (fixing the mind with effort on the object of comtemplation) is esteemed higher than knowledge."

The Sanskrit words are *jnana* and *dhyana* which are ordinarily translated as *knowledge* and *contemplation* respectively. Now *knowledge* is a very comprehensive term including various kinds and degrees from a *simple cognition* to the highest *comparative knowledge*. The *knowledge* here referred to is *dharana* (grasp) *i.e.* grasp of an object by attention, while *contemplation* implies a continuity of attention to consider the object in all its aspects.

"In Book vii. 16-18, four classes of good men

are mentioned. It is said, 'All these are noble. But the man possessed of knowledge is deemed by Me to be My own self.'"

The translation is not felicitous, but we would not mind it in trying to explain the verses. The four classes of *good workers* (*not* simply *good men*) are (1) the distressed, (2) the wisdom-seeking, (3) the wealth-seeking and (4) the wise. This last is held to be even "Mine own self" *i.e.* very intimate or dear to Me, because, as ver. 18 says, the wise man being righteous (*yukta*) and devoted to the One loves "Me" above every object (wealth, enjoyment or heavenly bliss). The indispensable groundwork is *good action*. When a doer of good serves God for relief from personal misery, he is a devotee of the 1st class; when for enlightenment, he is of the 2nd class; when for personal happiness, here or hereafter, he is of the

3rd class; when without any personal aim and simply from love of God above every object of personal desire, he is of the 4th class. The word *knowledge* does not adequately characterise the devotee of the 4th Class, but the verse describes him in terms which cannot be mistaken.

"At Gita, Chapter v. 15, it is said 'the Lord receives the sin or merit of none.' Yet at Chapter v. 29, and again at Chapter ix. 24, Krishna calls himself 'the Lord and enjoyer' of all sacrifices and penances. How, it may well be asked, can the Supreme Being 'enjoy' that which he does not even 'receive'?"

Assuming that 'Lord' in V. 15 means *God,* the sense of the quotation is that the Lord is not responsible for the *sin* or *merit* of any one, because man being a free agent acts on his own responsibility. God is not a director compelling him to make a particular choice so that sin or merit does not attach to Him, in the way in which the sin or merit of a servant's act attaches to his responsible human master. The word *bhoktaram*, used in V. 29 and IX. 24, means *enjoyer, protector* or *aider. Enjoyer* here signifies *approver* (as by tasting a thing). In any sense of *bhoktaram*, the idea conveyed in V. 15 is not inconsistent with it, as Mr. Telang, by a misinterpretation or a mere verbal interpretation, is led to think.

"9. THE SOUL."

"(1) *The Soul Eternal.*"—The examiner quotes II. 20, 24 and XV. 7, and says that if souls are eternal and self-existent, our relation with God is changed,—it becomes one of king and subjects, His right is then one of might, the loving relation of child to father disappears, and true religion is thus destroyed.

There is an evident reluctance to allow creature-souls a *past* eternity on the grounds set out. A *future* eternity is conceded, *absolutely* according to many, *conditionally* according to others. Human imagination being unrestricted in scope and variety, a multiplicity of hypotheses is inevitable in matters unverifiable by human reason and experience. The question, however now is, what is the doctrine of the Gita on this point? Adverting to VII. 4 and 5, we find mention of two *Prakritis* (Divine natures, or rather, powers): one manifests itself in the material Universe, the other in the creature-soul. Subject to this, is to be understood every other saying about the *soul* in the Gita. When, therefore, it is described as *unborn*, the idea of *physical* birth, implying chemical or organic changes in the formation and development of the foetus, is meant to be excluded. The substance of the soul is not liable to similar changes. XV. 7 seems to declare that the creature-soul is an eternal portion of "Me"; so that no change of the soul's relation with God is involved in the hypothesis that creature-souls are *eternal* and *unborn*.

"(2). *The Soul All-pervading.*"—The soul pervades all the body, each and every part of it. So far as human observation goes, all Universe is instinct with life, the life-principle pervades all space. In this sense the *soul* is held to be all-pervading. The allusion to the universal ubiquity of the mosquito's soul might well be spared. The allusion to the size of the soul might also be spared, unless, of course, the examiner honestly thought the Gita guilty of affirming extension, weight or some other *material* attribute as an attribute of the soul.

Philosophers are perplexed in hunting up adequate expressions to describe the soul; and when they say that the soul resides in the heart, or is subtle, or is infinitesimally small or is immeasurably vast, they simply make efforts to define it without offering the expressions as adequate definitions. The same may be said of many expressions in frequent use to indicate the grandeur and majesty of God. When, for example, upon hearing the saying, "Heaven is God's throne and the earth His footstool," one applies himself to ascertain the size of God's *foot* with his knowledge of the area of the earth's surface, he misses the pith of the saying.

"*(3) The Soul does not work, and is not*

stained."—The examiner refers with disapprobation to a *pandita's* argument about the soul's sinlessness, illustrated by the example of pure water and the contained dirt. It is well known that some substances are *soluble* in water, and some are only held *suspended* in it. The *pandita* might well say that the soul is *constitutionally pure* but sin may, like suspended matter in water, be found in it, and that any hypothesis, holding the nature of the soul to comprise a *constituent* element of sin, precludes the possibility of ever purifying it of sin. The Divine Will must then exert afresh to rebuild each soul with new material or substance.

The soul associated with mind and body is called *purusha;* and this *purusha,* being held to be susceptible to pleasure and pain, may approve or disapprove of the workings of the faculties and thus influence them. This is the doctrine of the Gita. The mind, it should be remembered, is simply a faculty or a medium and not the *soul* itself, according to the Gita.

"10. TRANSMIGRATION."

The examiner quotes II. 22, IV. 5, VI. 41, 42, and XVI. 19 and 20, and after describing the general Hindu belief in transmigration according to the laws of *Karma*, makes the following remarks:

"There is no doubt that the unequal distribution of happiness in this world is a problem which has exercised the minds of thinking men from the dawn of philosophy. On investigation, however, it will be seen that the doctrine of transmigration is attended with insuperable difficulties."

These (difficulties) we discuss below:

"*(1) It is contrary to our experience.*"— The examiner urges that, on the hypothesis, the body being alone changed and the mind with all its faculties continuing the same, the soul ought to carry with it a complete remembrance of its past history, but that no man has ever experienced anything of the kind. The examiner seems to ignore that events of early life are not at all remembered and that in old age the memory loses power, at times to such an extent as to excite mirth or pity. Instances are known of old men forgetting in a few minutes the personal act of having taken their usual meals. It cannot be said that even in this life we have a *complete* remembrance of our infancy. The examiner concludes with the remark, "we cannot recollect events of an alleged former birth because they had no existence." The argument, as put, would support the absurd theory that we had no infancy, or that no events occurred in it.

The Gita, II. 28, admits that the *past* of a man (before birth) is unknown, the future (after death) is undiscoverable, the existing life is thus the only basis of all speculations. To suppose a child born as the result of the mutual approach of two persons would not account for its possession of a soul, and as no effect is without a cause, the human mind is apt to speculate about it. It is argued that the cause in this case must be either the Divine Will acting on occasion of each and every birth, or a Divine Law, in pursuance of which the soul gets into the gross body. The former is held to be an irrational hypothesis. A child born in full health dies in 6 months. What trial does its soul undergo here? Another is a born leper who drags a *painful* existence for the full term of human life. Why so extraordinary a trial of his soul? A child born in the midst of thugs receives all the villainous education possible among them without an opportunity of acquiring moral ideas. Why is the soul put into his body so circumstanced? Instances can be multiplied, but the above are sufficient. The Hindu thinks the laws of Karma and transmigration account for this diversity to some extent.

"(2) *It is unjust.*"—The argument is as follows :—

"If a man is so changed at each birth as to forget all his previous history, he becomes virtually a new being. What he suffers now he suffers on account of sins committed by another; and these sufferings he has no choice but to endure. Even the very sins a man now commits are punishments of previous sins, and he cannot but commit them. Their punishment, again, he cannot bear in this life if he would; they must be borne by him in another birth, when the loss of all consciousness of the present has made him, in fact, another person. His present happiness is the reward of a previous person's good deeds, his present good deeds will be rewarded to some future person. In all this there is an absence of justice."

The argument confessedly has great force. But man cannot rest satisfied without thinking of the inequalities everyday met with, and is bound to devise an explanation which should exonerate God from the charge of injustice. The Hindu is not satisfied with the story about Adam's sin, and his bequeathing an *inherent* taint to all succeeding generations. The doctrine of transmigration, however, offers a more satisficatory explanation in that it holds good at least up to a link next after the first in the chain of successive lives. The doctrine is, however, a provisional hypothesis like the scaffolding which must be laid aside when the building is completed.

"(3) *It denies Divine Mercy.*"—The doctrine does indeed recognise Divine Justice as the paramount attribute of God. What Divine Justice is, is explained in IX. 29. If free grace is expected, sinning would be rampant in the world. Even Christianity sees the necessity of upholding Divine Justice. The sacrifice of Jesus whom God is said to have sent into the world as an act of grace is held to have the effect of reconciling the two, Justice and Mercy. But this Mercy is contingent on one's free will confessing Jesus as Christ, and thus the annexment of this condition refunds to Divine Justice whatever of hardship was sought to be taken away by the doctrine of Divine Mercy. The Gita says that God is just in serving whosoever serves Him (IX. 29), that serving God consists in serving His creatures, in relieving their misery and promoting their happiness (VI. 31 and 32).

The treatment of lepers and widows among Hindus is incidentally alluded to as being unkind under the influence of this doctrine. The charge of general unkindness is unfounded. Particular instances of unkind treatment are due, not to the doctrine of transmigration, but to the individual character and dispositions, as in every other country, of those who are guilty of it.

"(4) *Its effects* are pernicious."—It is argued that, when people believe their misfortunes arise from sins in a former birth, they rest contented and make no efforts to remove them. To some extent this may be true, but the same doctrine holds out a hope of reward in the next life, and ought to offer no small incentive to laudable activity. The real mischief is due neither to this doctrine; nor to that doctrine, but to general indolence which is the cause as well as the effect of ignorant priestly influence in India.

Other objections to the doctrine of transmigration:

"(*i*) *Inequalities of happiness are less than is supposed.* —There are many poor men far happier than the rich. "Wealth and power are, not unfrequently, a curse rather than a blessing." We admit that men often make false estimates of happiness; but what have these to do with this doctrine any more than they have to do with any other doctrine indisputably true?

"(*ii*) *It promotes worldliness.*"— Because, it is said, it holds out the hope of virtue being rewarded by bodily health, by wealth, lands, comfort, etc. The value of this argument is not understood. You may as well say that human energy is not good because it is calculated to accelerate the speed of a fall. The value of the Baconian philosophy and method is extolled on account of the "fruit" obtainable. Why then, has the transmigration theory, fostering the hope of such reward, not given impulse to scientific activity in India?

"(*iii*) *We can look forward as well as backward*—This world is a state of preparation for the next. Like a child at school you are being disciplined for purposes of life. Even with all the pain and sorrow in the world, you are too much attached to it. Much more would be the case if all went right with you." We have nothing to say against the above, nor even against the hopes entertained of relatives meeting in the next world, whether it be an enlightened *Pitriloka,* or a *Devaloka,* or any other of the *many* compartments which our Great Father has in his house.

"11. MUKTI, THE GREAT AIM OF THE BHAGAVAD GITA."

VIII. 15, and IX. 20, 21 declare that this world is "the seat of pain and death; even the happiness of heaven is only transient." The examiner says, "How to get rid of the curse of existence and not to be born again, is the grand object."

The word *existence* has been used in the above in some sense which the reader of the Gita may not well appreciate. By *birth* is always meant *birth into mortal nature,* for which one need have no great predilection if he understand his real interest. Whether transmigration, or the Purgatory, or some other hypothesis is the better, cannot be the object of scientific proof, and as Revelation or imagination is the origin of diverse hypotheses according to diversity of hope and desires, the jurisdiction of reason is necessarily excluded in these matters.

The examiner thinks with the Vedanta philosophers that *mukti,* according to the Gita, means *absorption* in the Deity; and he argues that, God being different from any other being, *absorption* is impossible, and, if assumed to be possible, it amounts practically to *annihilation,* the Hindu Brahma being in a state of dreamless sleep without any more thought than a stone. The following have been cited in support of his interpretation: IV. 9; VI. 15, 27 VIII. 12, 13; XIV. 19 and XVIII. 54, 55; also IX. 34 and XI. 55. These are not properly construed or carefully translated; thus—

In IV. 9, *mam eti* translated *entereth into Me* instead of *comes to Me*.

In VI. 15, *Nirvana* is left untranslated to allow of its being held to signify the Buddhistic *nirvana;* whereas it signifies the *quenching of fire or of the worldly desires* (III. 39) *which rage like fire,* or, in short, it means *tranquillity of mind.*

In VI. 27, *Brahma bhutam* is rendered *is one with Brahma,* whereas *Brahma-natured, eventempered* or *just* would be appropriate. (*Samam* is also Brahma).

In XIV. 19, *Adhigachchhati* is translated *entercth into* instead of *attains to* or *reaches.*

Madhhavam is translated *My being* instead of *My nature* or *My dispositions, i.e., godly perfection.*

In XVIII. 54 and 55, *Brahmabhuta*

mistranslated as in VI. 27, notwithstanding the 2nd line of ver. 54 points to a further step in progress (*supreme devotion*). The expression 'entereth into My *essence*' is justified nothing in the original. *Tadanantaram* signifies *then,* or *that the inseparate, i.e., My perfection* or *My nature*.

It will be seen how the examiner by using misleading equivalents of Sanskrit words develops the theory of *absorption*. VIII. 12 and 13, IX. 34 and XI. 55 prove nothing on this point, while the whole tenor of the Gita leaves no room for mistaking its real doctrine.

The examiner admits that some Vaishnavas look for a future-conscious existence with Vishnu, but adds that this is not according to the teaching of the Hindu Scriptures. That this is not contrary to the teachings of the Gita has been already alluded to. The examiner then goes on to say, "Besides, there is no such being as Vishnu," as if the word, which conveys the idea of *all-pervading* or *omnipresent,* is not worthy enough.

"12. ENCOURAGEMENT OF YOGA EXERCISES."

The examiner begins operations with a quotation (II. 49), "action is far inferior to the devotion of the mind." A more literal translation is "The act is far inferior to the Yoga of the understanding." Ver. 48, according to the translation in the missionary pamphlet, is "abandon all thought of the consequence, and make the event equal, whether it terminate in good or evil; for such an equality is called *Yoga.*" *Yoga* is thus the *mental equipoise* or *rectitude* which, irrespective of the consideration of success or failure, dictates an act and gives it the character of *duty*. Bearing this interpretation of *Yoga* in mind, one cannot fail to see that ver. 49 means to compare the values of the *outer act* and the *inner sense,* and assign a higher worth to the latter. In other words, it declares that it is the *inner* motive which justifies the *outer act.* So far *Yoga* does not import anything reprehensible.

The examiner follows the reference to II. 49 with a discourse about Patanjala Yoga and various Yoga postures supposed to be those meant by Patanjali, and arrives at the conclusion that the Gita sees the need of action, but, on the whole, teaches that 'work is far inferior to the devotion of the mind.' It will be unnecessary to point out that his conclusion is based upon an inadequate interpretation of II. 49.

He then refers to IV. 29, V. 26, VI. 10-

15, and seeks to prove that the Gita approves the Yoga exercises, prescribed by Patanjali, which end in a state of inanition. The Gita does indeed enumerate certain conditions favourable to the contemplation of the Divine Representative and the formation of a tranquil frame of mind freed from the disturbances of the desires and passions. The object, as pointed out later on, is to mentally realise and then acquire Brahma-nature or perfection for Patanjala Yoga, (perhaps under a misapprehension of its scope and meaning,) furnishes no fair ground for putting a strained construction on passages of the Gita. What are the usual symptoms of a man in deep thought? his gaze is fixed, rather vacantly, his breathing becomes slow and even, his posture stiff, his mind fixed and not easily liable to be disturbed. It is undeniable that solitude, and easy posture without violent movements of the limbs, consequent even regular breathing, avoiding distractions from objects of sight, etc.,—all these favour attentive pondering on any subject.

It is said that Yoga exercises, "conscientiously observed, can only issue in folly and idiocy." Without trying to ascertain what "conscientious observance" of Yoga exercise is, it would be profitable to enquire what the Gita aims at. The production of a continuous passive state of the mind is *not* its aim as is generally supposed, but it is to educate one for right thinking, right feeling, and right acting (VI. 29-32). A quotation from an eminent minister of religion dilates on the meagre results of the teachings of the Gita. He ought to remember Jesus's saying about the meagre result from the good word in unsuitable soil. The great master failed to make any impression on the intelligent Jews, and had to resort to miraculous doings to attract fishermen and other ignorant people. The influence of Christianity is said to have contributed to the development of the Baconian philosophy and method. To some extent this may be true, but at the same time it is no less true that, generally, the professed ministers and exponents of that religion never failed to impede scientific progress.

"13. ACTIONS PERFORMED WITHOUT ATTACHMENT (SANGA) DO NOT 'DEFILE.'"

The examiner gives a rambling discourse on this point, and offers nothing definite to get hold of. It is meant apparently for a reflection on the conduct of an Akulkote *Sadhu* and Swami Vivekananda, which has little to do with the Gita. One object of the discourse seems to be to show that Krishna by this teaching sought to induce Arjuna to *kill* his relations. The proposition is put rather pointedly and in an objectionably incomplete form; but it must be confessed that Krishna wanted to impress on the mind of Arjuna the paramount character of *duty* which, irrespective of personal feelings and motives, should be performed though it involved the *killing* of relations. No spiritual guide would be blamed for giving similar advice under similar circumstances, as, for example, to a Wellington before Waterloo, if found overpowered and confounded by sentiments of incongruous pity.

"14. CASTE ALLEGED TO BE A DIVINE INSTITUTION."

Social classification follows a natural law, and differs in form under different circumstances. In India the fourfold classification was founded mainly upon the colour of the skin, special aptitude for special functions, and heredity. Krishna found it as a social fact, and held it was not accidental. He attributed it (IV. 13) to a natural law (or, otherwise put, Divine Will), causing an assortment according to personal dispositions and activity. As in an organized State, there are departments of War, Revenue, Agriculture, Civil Justice, the Police, etc., and the members of each department are specially qualified and held bound to perform the duties of that department, so the pronounced form which the social organization had assumed in Krishna's time consisted, as it were, of four departments for the discharge of social and political functions, the distribution of which was regulated by recognising certain class qualifications and class duties. It is doubtful if the system was as inelastic then as it is now; and though heredity could not fail to be an important factor in settling a man's status, yet the fact is not without significance that Krishna's stay, in the midst of Vaishyas of the lowest class, for many years, entailed no forfeiture of his Kshatriya status. His own doctrine gives greater prominence to natural parts (XVIII. 41-44), while in spiritual matters it recognised no distinctions (IX. 32, 33). What the Gita means is that classification in society is natural and also good, and it refers to the fourfold race-colour as the system in actual existence. If one were to say that God created the white man, the red man, the yellow man and the dark man with their respective characteristic aptitudes, of which the distinctions were undeniable at the time, the proposition would hardly be false. Even now when considerable changes have taken place in social structures in different countries, class distinctions upon some principle or other are not wanting. Krishna could not ignore the caste system, but took care to point out what its real essence or scope was.

III. 24 has been mistranslated by assigning to *sankara* the meaning of *varnasankara*. Read with the preceding and following verses, III. 24 must be held to point out the consequences of the renunciation of activity by representative men. The able-bodied physical labourer would give up his legitimate work, and imitate the physical idleness of the intellectual worker. A misapplication of characteristic abilities would thus necessarily result in a wholesale deterioration of the society. III. 24 has nothing to do with caste mixtures.

Social classification, as already stated, is natural and advantageous. The circumstances of early Hindu society developed it into a certain form, and this form, by the very nature of things, as foreseen by Rishis of old, cannot subsist for ever. Its decay is inevitable, and it must give place to some other on a principle more suited to the times. If the Gita upheld the form existing in its time because it was still suitable with some suggested modifications, it is not fair criticism to blame the Gita because the present altered circumstances of Hindu Society are supposed to call for a classification on a different principle.

"15. THE EFFICACY OF SHRADDHAS."

I. 42, quoted in support, is Arjuna's saying in regard to which there is not a single word from the mouth of the Teacher. (*Vide* Notes). To cherish the memory of a deceased parent by some formal expression cannot be blamed. The abuse of an institution is no ground for its abolition if the institution itself be good and the abuse can be avoided.

"16. THE VALUE OF BHAKTI."

The examiner after citing IX. 30 and XVIII. 71, says:—

"The value of faith depends upon its object. Faith in an imaginary being who has no existence must be worthless, and can only destroy him by whom it is exercised. The Krishna of the Bhagavad Gita is a mere fiction of the Vaishnava Brahmin by whom it was written. Faith in Krishna, as described in the Puranas, with 16,100 wives, would be still worse."

It is enough that *bhakti* is conceded to be good. *Avatars* are *no longer visible* to us, and, from good or bad motives, their biographers have failed to represent them properly in every country. At least it becomes necessary to eliminate stupid or caricaturing narrations from friendly and hostile writings, and form an *ideal* for ourselves. *Bhakti* cannot then do mischief, so long as reason is free to check extravagances of imagination, credulity and prejudice.

"17. KNOWLEDGE REDUCES SIN TO ASHES."

The examiner cites IV. 36 and 37 and asks, "What is the knowledge that has such effects? The blasphemous assertion, *Aham Brahma*, I am God. Is this true or false?"

It is not necessary to answer his 2nd query but only to point out that the answer he gives to his first question is not a proper answer. The immediately preceding verse

(35) describes the knowledge or wisdom to be one which enables its possessor to understand the identity in nature and the identity in Parentage of all men, or, in other words, the Fatherhood of God and the brotherhood of man.

"18. DYING IN THE LIGHT AND DARK FORTNIGHTS."

The examiner after referring to VIII. 23-25 says: "Does any intelligent man believe that his future happiness depends upon his dying in the light or dark fortnight?" The answer, of course, is in the negative. But do the verses raise the question? Assuming that the verses should be literally understood, they declare that Brahma-knowers go to Brahma treading a path characterized by luminousness which increases in volume and duration during their onward progress, and that profit-seeking workers, treading another path characterized by darkness increasing in volume and duration, obtain lunar (dim) light and then revert. Would the converse of propositions be necessarily true? If not, how is the question relevant, unless, perhaps, the examiner has been influenced by the story of Bhishma's dying in a particular season? That story has nothing to do with the verses under discussion. They simply seek to describe in metaphorical language the characters of two imaginary paths which the wise man and the profit-seeking worker respectively take after death in their journeys to their respective destinations. In other words, the God-loving and the pleasure-loving travel after death on different paths, ever distinguished by the epithets *light* and *dark*.

In discussing the points noticed in the

Examination, no attempt has been made to deal with observations on popular Hindu opinions and beliefs, for which the Gita is no responsible.

In this connexion it may be well to advert to a startling observation made by a distinguished Director of Public Instruction after perusal of the Gita. He cannot "resist the conviction that a vein of insincerity runs through this exhortation." Such a novel opinion can only be the result of careless reading or bias, for the Gita nowhere speaks in parables with a view to preclude unsympathizers from comprehending its teachings; and if it makes large concessions to each and every theological or philosophical doctrine then current, it is because each has some truth at its basis, and errs only on account of its narrowness. Human life is a compound of thought, feeling and activity, and any philosophy or theology, which overlooks their inter-dependence and the fluctuations in their relative influences at different periods of life, is apt to build its theory upon a narrow foundation with the result that it can satisfy only a limited class or sect. The Gita is, however, more catholic. It allows *thinking, feeling, and willing* to have their respective predominating influences in succession at different periods of life and adjust themselves accordingly in relative subordination or co-ordination, differently, indeed, in different individuals, under the ruling idea of DUTY or loving obedience to GOD, indicated by the teachings and example of the model man or GOD'S REPRESENTATIVE OF THE AGE.

GITA FOR EVERYONE

CHAPTER I

Despondency

Dhritarashtra said : O Sanjaya, what did mine and Pandu's sons do, gathered together ready for fight on the Holy Plain, on Kurukshetra ?

2. Sanjaya said: seeing the Pandava army arrayed, Raja Duryodhana approaching his preceptor uttered himself thus:—

3. Behold, O Teacher, this grand army of Pandu's sons, arrayed by the sapient disciple, the son of Drupada.

4. Herein are heroes, great bowmen equal to Bhima and Arjuna in battle, Yuyudhana, Virata, Drupada the great car-warrior,

5. Dhrishtaketu, Chekitana, Kashi's mighty King, Purujit, Kuntibhoja, Shaivya the bull among men,

6. Yudhamanyu the valiant, Uttamauja the strong, Subhadra's son, and Draupadi's sons, all, indeed, great car-warriors.

7. Mark also, O highest of the twice-born, those that are distinguished among us, the leaders of my army. These I describe for thy information:

8. Thyself, Bhishma, Kripa the vanquisher in battle, Ashwatthama, Vikarna, Somadatta's son Jayadratha;

9. And many other heroes, regardless of life for my sake, armed with divers destructive weapons, all skilled in warfare.

10. This force of ours, commanded by Bhishma, is imperfect, but that force

of theirs, commanded by Bhima,
is perfect.

11. Therefore, stationed in respective
divisions at all the passage, do ye all
protect Bhishma alone.

12. Cheering him up, the eldest of the
Kurus, the glorious grandsire, loudly
vociferating blew his conch.

13. Then conches, trumpets, *turis,
anakas* and *gomukhas* at once blared
forth. The sound was terrible.

14. Then seated on their great car,
drawn by white horses, Madhava and
Pandava blew their splendid conches;

15. Hrishikesha, the *panchajanya;*
Dhananjaya, the *devadatta.* Vrikodara,
the terrible in action, blew his enormous
conch, the *paundra;*

16. The Raja, Kunti's son
Yudhishthira, the *anantabijaya,* Nakula

and Sahadeva, the *sughosha* and *manipushpaka* (respectively).

17. The superior bowman Kashya, the great car-warrior Shikhandi, Dhrishtadyumna, Virata, the unvanquished Satyaki,

18. Drupada, Draupadi's sons, and Subhadra's mighty-armed son, O King of Earth, blew their respective conches from all sides.

19. That dreadful noise, reverberating through earth and sky, pierced the hearts of Dhritarashtra's sons.

20. Thus beholding Dhritarashtra's party severally stationed, the ape-bannered Pandava, O King, taking up his bow when the fight was about to begin, then addressed Hrishikesha thus:—

21. Arjuna said: "Betwixt both armies

stay my car, O unfallen one.

22. "While I behold these, standing eager for a fight, who confront me at the commencement of this war;

23. "And have a look at these, that, ready for fight, have gathered to the battle as well-wishers of the wrong-minded son of Dhritarashtra."

24. Sanjaya said: Thus addressed by Gudakesha, O Bharata, Hrishikesha staying the best of cars betwixt both armies,

25. Over against Bhishma, Drona, and all the rulers of earth, said "O Partha, behold these, the Kurus assembled."

26. There in both armies alike, Partha saw stationed fathers and grandfathers, preceptors, maternal uncles, brothers, sons, grandsons, comrades, fathers-in-law and friends.

27. Finding all these relatives thus waiting, the son of Kunti moved by common pity said thus desponding:—

28. Arjuna said: Seeing these kinsmen standing ready for fight, O Krishna, my limbs fail, and my mouth is parched;

29. My body trembles and my hair stands on end, Gandiva slips from my hand, and my skin, too, burns all over;

30. Nor am I able to stand, and my mind is, as it were, whirling, and I see adverse signs, O Keshava;

31. Nor do I foresee good after slaying kinsmen in battle, O Krishna; I desire neither victory, nor sovereignty, nor pleasures.

32. What, O Govinda, is sovereignty to us? What, enjoyments? or even life? Those for whose sake are desired sovereignty, enjoyments, and pleasures,

33. Even they, regardless of life and wealth, are standing in battle,— preceptors, fathers, sons, and grandfathers,

34. Maternal uncles, father-in-law, grandsons, brothers-in-law, and (other) relatives. These, O Madhusudana, I wish not to slay though (I be) slain;

35. Not even for the sake of sovereignty over the triple world. How then for gaining the Earth? What satisfaction would be ours by killing Dhritarashtra's sons?

36. Sin will even overtake us by our killing these felons. Therefore we should not kill Dhritarashtra's sons with their relatives. Indeed, how can we be happy after killing kinsmen, O Madhava?

37. Although these with greed-

overpowered minds see not the evil of causing family-decay nor the sin of harming friends,

38. Should not we, who realize the sin of extirpating our race, avoid such sin, O Janardana?

39. With the decline of a race its ancient morality dies out. The morality extinct, immorality overcomes the whole race.

40. Overcome by immorality, O Krishna, the women of the race become corrupt. The women becoming corrupt, the whole race grows tainted.

41. The taint leads but to hell the racedestroyers and the race; for, their forefathers fall off, losing the offerings of food and drink.

42. By these crimes of race-destroyers, productive of a tainted race,

are abolished the enduring morality of the nation and of the race.

43. Of men whose family morality has perished, O Janardana, the abode in hell is lasting. Thus have we heard.

44. Alas! a great sin are we resolved upon committing when ready to kill kinsmen from greed of the pleasures of sovereignty.

45. For me it would be the better if Dhritarashtra's sons in battle, weapon in hand, slew me unresisting and unarmed.

46. Sanjaya said: Having thus spoken, Arjuna, casting aside his bow and arrow in grief-overwhelmed mind, dropped down on his car-seat in the battle (field).

Thus in the Upanishad of the Glorious Divine Lay, the Science of Brahma, the Ordinance of Yoga, the Discourse between the Glorious

Krishna and Arjuna, the First chapter entitled "the Despondency of Arjuna."

CHAPTER II
The Sankhya Yoga

Sanjaya said: To him thus overcome with pity, desponding with tearful troubled eyes, these words spoke Madhusudana:—

2. The Glorious Lord said: Whence at this crisis, O Arjuna, has come unto thee this dejection, suited to non-Aryans, heaven-closing, and disreputable?

3. O Partha, yield not to impotence. That does not befit thee. Stand up, shake off paltry faint-heartedness, O dismayer of foes.

4. Arjuna said: How, in battle, O Madhusudana, O slayer of foes, shall I fight the venerable Bhishma and Drona with arrows?

5. For, instead of killing elders of high character, it is better to live upon alms in this world. By killing (such) elders, we shall have, even here, to taste the enjoyments of blood-stained wealth and luxury.

6. Nor do I know which is the better for us—"we conquer" or "they conquer us." Those whom after slaying we care not to survive, even they, Dhritarashtra's sons, stand opposed to us.

7. My nature overcome by the evil of narrowness, my mind bewildered as to righteousness, I ask Thee, tell me decisively that which is good. I am Thy disciple suppliant at Thy feet; instruct me.

8. For I can find nothing that would assuage my sense-withering grief, even though I were to attain unrivalled and

prosperous monarchy on earth or sovereignty over the gods.

9. Sanjaya said: Having thus addressed Hrishikesha, Gudakesha the dismayer of foes, saying to Govinda "I will not fight," became silent.

10. To him, despondent in the midst of both armies, O Bharata, Hrishikesha, as if smiling, spoke these words:

11. The Glorious Lord said: Thou grievest for those unworthy of thy grief, and speakest words of wisdom. The wise grieve neither for the dead nor for the living.

12. Indeed, there never was a time when I was not, nor thou, nor these chiefs of men. Neither in the hereafter shall we ever cease to be.

13. As the Embodied One leaves childhood, youth, and old age in this

body, so he leaves this body (itself). The reflective man is not confounded at this.

14. Sense-contacts, O son of Kunti, are givers of heat and cold, pleasure and pain; they come and pass away and are (thus) impermanent. Patiently bear them, O Bharata.

15. The man, equable in pleasure and pain and reflective, whom these cannot afflict, is fitted for immortality, O mighty Bharata.

16. Certainty of the Unreal can never be, nor can uncertainty be of the Real. Even (thus) have truth-discerners seen the limit between these two.

17. Now, know that to be indestructible, whereby all this is pervaded. None can effect the destruction of this Imperishable.

18. Finite are said to be the bodies of

the Embodied One (Who is Himself) permanent, indestructible, and not knowable by argument (but by intuition). Therefore fight, O Bharata.

19. He who thinks it is This that slays, and he who thinks it is This that is slain, are both ill-instructed. This neither slays nor is slain.

20. This is not born nor dies, nor, having once been, again ceases to be. Unborn, permanent, everlasting, ancient-and-fresh, This is not slain on the body being slaughtered.

21. The man that knows This as indestructible, permanent, unborn, and undiminishing, how and whom, O Partha, can that man slay or cause to be slain?

22. As a man, casting off worn-out garments, takes others that are new, so

the Embodied One casting off worn-out bodies, goes into other new ones.

23. This neither weapons cleave, nor fire burns, nor waters wet, nor wind dries up.

24. Uncleavable is This, incombustible This, and indeed neither liable to be wetted nor dried up. Perpetual, all-pervading, stable, immoveable, and immemorial is This. Unperceived is This, unimaginable is This, immutable is This said to be.

25. Therefore, knowing This to be such, thou shouldst not grieve.

26. If, however, thou thinkest This as being perpetually born or as perpetually dying, even then, O Mighty-armed, thou shouldst not thus grieve.

27. For sure is the death of what is born, and sure is the birth of what is

dead. Therefore, over the inevitable result thou shouldst not grieve.

28. Creatures have an unknown origin, a manifest middle state and also an unknown future, O Bharata. Why then lament?

29. Some one sees This as marvellous and likewise another describes (This) as marvellous, and indeed none, even having heard (the Shruti), understands This.

30. The Embodied is ever invulnerable in every one's body, O Bharata. Therefore, for no creatures shouldst thou grieve.

31. Looking also upon thine own duty, thou shouldst not falter; for, to a Kshatriya, nothing else is better than righteous war.

32. Happy the Kshatriyas, O Partha,

who obtain such a fight, come unsought like the heaven's gate unclosed.

33. If, however, this righteous warfare, thou carriest not on, then, falling off from thy duty and fame, thou wilt incur sin.

34. Moreover, people will even proclaim thy undying infamy; and infamy to a noble is worse than death.

35. The great car-warriors will think fear makes thee shrink from fight; and, after having been highly esteemed by them, thou wilt be lightly held.

36. Thine enemies will utter many reproachful words, slandering thy prowess. What more painful than that?

37. Either, killed, thou wilt obtain heaven; or, victorious, thou wilt enjoy the Earth. Therefore, stand up, O son of Kunti, resolved upon war.

38. Equally prepared for pleasure and pain, gain and loss, victory and defeat, then prepare thyself for fight. Thus thou shalt not incur sin.

39. This, explained to thee, is wisdom according to the Sankhya method. Hear now this (other) according to the Yoga, with the help of which wisdom thou wilt cast off the trammels of action, O Partha.

40. In this there is no loss of progress, nor is there retrogression. Even a little of this righteousness rescues from great fear.

41. In this the right deliberate understanding is one and single, O son of the Kurus. The understandings of the indeliberate are many-branched and endless.

42. The unreflective, O Partha, fond

of the word of the Vedas, and saying "nothing else is (behind the word)," utter this the flowery speech,

43. Which offers birth and fruit of actions and abounds with various special acts towards the attainment of gratification and lordship, they being full of desire and esteeming as the highest goal the heaven (of selfish gratification).

44. For these, (thus) fond of gratification and lordship, and robbed of their minds by that (speech), the right understanding is not ordained on firm basis.

45. The Vedas have for their object the attribute-triad. Be thou, O Arjuna, uninfluenced by the attribute-triad, uninfluenced by the duals, settled in permanent goodness, unmindful

of acquisition and preservation and self-possessed.

46. Whatever the use of an all-flooding water for drinking, the same is that of all the Vedas to a well-informed devotee of Brahma.

47. Thy power of action extends to the act never to its fruit. Seek not for action-fruit. Have no attachment to inaction.

48. Settled in Yoga do thou perform action; O Dhananjaya, renouncing attachment and being equipoised for success and failure (This) equipoise is called Yoga.

49. Far inferior to this Yoga of the understanding is action, O Dhananjaya. Seek shelter in this understanding. Pitiable are the fruit-seekers.

50. One, aided by (this) understand-

ing, is here unaffected by acts whether well-performed or ill-performed. Therefore cling to Yoga. Yoga is the felicity in action.

51. Renouncing the action-born fruit and being completely liberated from the bonds of birth, sages endued with (this) understanding repair to the healthy goal.

52. When thy understanding shall have transcended the mazes of bewilderment, then shalt thou obtain a clear knowledge of what thou wilt hear or hast heard.

53. When well-informed by hearing, thy understanding will stand unmoving and firm on a perfect basis, then shalt thou attain to Yoga.

54. Arjuna said: What, O Keshava, is meant by "a man of stable understanding settled on a firm basis"?

How does the man of stable understanding talk? How sit? How move?

55. The Glorious Lord said: When, O Partha, one rejects all objective desires of the mind, satisfied by the self in the self alone, then is he said to be of stable understanding.

56. One whose mind is unagitated amidst pains, who has no hankering amidst pleasures, whose likings, fears and anger have passed away, he of stable understanding is called a Muni.

57. When without attaching himself to anything he, getting good and evil by turns, neither exults nor hates, then is his understanding settled.

58. When from sense-objects on all sides he can draw in the senses as a tortoise its limbs, then is his

understanding settled.

59. Sense-objects, but not the taste (for them), turn away from the abstaining Embodied One. The Supreme seen, his taste also turns away.

60. O son of Kunti, the tyrannical senses forcibly carry away the will of even a cautious reflective man.

61. (Therefore) restraining them all, one settled in Yoga should sit aiming at Me as the highest goal; for his understanding remains settled whose senses are kept under control.

62. In a man musing on objects attachment to them is conceived. From attachment springs desire; from desire springs wrath;

63. From wrath is utter confoundedness; from utter confoundedness, whirling memory; from loss of memory, the

loss of the understanding; from loss of the understanding he perishes.

64. But when his self obeys rule, he moving amid objects with senses deprived of affection and antipathy and subservient to the self, attains to cheerfulness.

65. There being cheerfulness, the extinction of all his pains follows; for the understanding of the cheerful-minded soon becomes thoroughly settled.

66. One unsettled in Yoga has not (this) understanding; nor has one, unsettled in Yoga, reflection; nor has the unreflective man tranquillity; Where is happiness for the untranquillized?

67. The mind, which follows the dictates of the roving senses, draws away his understanding just as a gale a boat in waters.

68. Therefore, O mighty-armed, his understanding remains settled, whose senses are withdrawn from the objects of the senses all round.

69. In that which is the night of all creatures, the restrainer is awake. When (all other) creatures wake, that is the night for the discerning *Muni*.

70. He gains peace, into whom desires flow as waters flow into the ever-filling unchangeable ocean,—not he that is a seeker of desires.

71. That man who, shaking off all desires, goes on yearningless, considering nothing as his own, and unegoistic, he attains peace.

72. The state, O Partha, of being established in Brahma is this. One attaining thereto is not liable to bewilderment, and, settled therein

even at the last moment, gets repose
in Brahma.

Thus in the Upanishad of the Glorious Divine
Lay, the Science of Brahma, the Ordinance of
Yoga, the Discourse between the Glorious
Krishna and Arjuna, the Second Chapter
entitled "The Sankhya Yoga."

THE SANKHYA YOGA

Lay, the Science of Brahma, the Ordinance of
Yoga, the Discourse between the Glorious

CHAPTER III

Action Yoga.

Arjuna said: If Thou, O Janardana, thinkest knowledge is greater than action, then why dost Thou, O Keshava, enjoin on me action that is dreadful?

2. By intermingled precepts, as it were, Thou art bewildering my understanding. Declare decidedly that one by which I may obtain good.

3. The Glorious Lord said: In this world there is a two-fold path already declared by Me, O sinless one,—that of the Sankhyas by the Yoga of knowledge, and that of the Yogis by the Yoga of action.

4. Man cannot enjoy respite from activity by non-undertaking of

actions, nor can he obtain success by surrendering them.

5. No one can remain inactive even for a moment; for, impotent through nature-sprung attributes, every one is forced to act.

6. He who, controlling the organs of action, sits musing in mind on the objects of the senses, he is called a hypocrite who deludes himself.

7. But he who, regulating his senses by the will, O Arjuna, commences the Yoga of action with the organs of action, he, becoming unattached, excels.

8. Do thou perform nature-ordained action; for action is greater than inaction. Even thy journey in this body will not be possible with inaction.

9. But this world will be clogged by action unless it be action for the sake of

sacrifice. For the sake thereof, O son of Kunti, free from attachment, perform thou action.

10. The Lord of offspring, having in olden time created offspring with sacrifice, said: "Hereby grow. Be this the dispenser of your cherished desires.

11. "Hereby support the gods, the gods will support you. In supporting one another do ye attain to the Supreme Good.

12. "The sacrifice-supported gods will certainly bestow on you cherished enjoyments. He who enjoys their gifts without giving them in return is a thief indeed."

13. The righteous, eating at the completion of sacrifice, are freed from all sins; but it is sin that the sinful taste, who cook (only) for their own sake.

14. From food come creatures into being, the production of food is from showers, showers spring from sacrifice, sacrifice is action-produced;

15. Know action sprung from Brahma, Brahma sprung from the Imperishable. Hence the all-pervading Brahma is ever abiding in sacrifice.

16. He who follows not the wheel thus set rolling, he of sinful life, the sense-gratified, lives in vain, O Partha.

17. But the man who is really devoted to the self, and is satisfied with the self, and remains contented with the self, he has nothing to do.

18. For him, indeed, there would be no interest in what is done, nor any here in what is not done; for, no interest of his is dependent on any creature.

19. Therefore, unattached, always

perform action which should be done; for man by performing (such) action without attachment attains to the Supreme.

20. By action, indeed, Janaka and others obtained success. In view also of popular community thou shouldst perform action.

21. Whatever a superior man does, the inferior man also does: people follow that which he makes as the standard.

22. There is nothing, O Partha, for Me to do, nor is there anything unattained in the triple-world to attain, still I move amid action.

23. For if ever I moved not watchfully amid action, men would follow My path, O Partha, from all sides.

24. These worlds would fall into ruin if I performed not action. I should also

become the author of deterioration, and should ruin these creatures.

25. As attached to action, O Bharata, the unwise act, so unattached the wise should act, desirous of holding the masses together.

26. One should not unsettle the understanding of the ignorant who are attached to action. The wise man, acting Yoga-settled, should create inducement to all actions.

27. Acts are fully done by the attributes of nature. One whose self is deluded by egoism thinks "I am the actor."

28. But, O mighty-armed, the knower of the truth regarding the attribute-group and the function-group, holding that attributes move amid attributes, becomes unattached.

29. Those that are deluded by the attributes of nature are attached to the functions of the attributes. The perfect knower should not unsettle such dull imperfect knowers.

30. Surrendering all action unto Me with the mind fixed on the Ruling self, becoming inexpectant, and thinking nothing as thine own, do thou fight, rid of (mental) fever.

31. Those men that always abide in this My injunction, full of faith and alacrity, do, even by actions, find liberation.

32. But they who disliking it abide not in My injunction, know thou these fools are ruined, being deluded in all knowledge.

33. Even the wise man exerts conformably to his nature. Creatures

must follow nature. What shall restraint avail?

34. The liking and disliking of a sense regarding the object of that sense are fixed. One should not come under their power, for they are his adversaries on the way.

35. One's own characteristic duty, bereft of its merit, is better (for him) than another's characteristic duty well done. Death in the midst of one's own duty is preferable. The duty which is another's is attended with risk.

36. Arjuna said: But, by what impelled, does man commit sin, even against his will, O Varshneya, and as if by force impelled?

37. The Glorious Lord said: It is desire, it is wrath, the offspring of the Passion-attribute, all-devouring, highly

sinful. Know this to be *the* enemy here.

38. As a flame is enveloped in smoke, as a mirror by dust, as an embryo by the womb, so is this (reason) enveloped thereby.

39. The reason of a rational being is enveloped by this persistent enemy, O son of Kunti, in the form of covetousness, a fire insatiable.

40. The senses, the will, and the understanding are said to be the seats thereof. Enveloping reason with these, it confounds the Embodied One.

41. Therefore, O mighty Bharata, bringing the senses first under control, do thou cast off this cause of sin, destructive, indeed, of perception and reason.

42. The senses are said to be superior, the will superior to the senses, the

understanding superior to the will, but what is superior to the understanding is That.

43. Having thus understood what is superior to the understanding, controlling the self by the self, do thou cast off, O Mighty-armed, the enemy in the form of desire, difficult to grasp.

Thus, in the Upanishad of the Glorious Divine Lay, the Science of Brahma, the Ordinance of Yoga, the Discourse between the Glorious Krishna and Arjuna, the Third Chapter entitled "The Action Yoga."

CHAPTER IV

The Wisdom Yoga

The Glorious Lord said: This unperishing Yoga I explained to Vivaswan, Vivaswan explained to Manu, Manu explained to Ikshvaku.

2. The king-sages knew this, thus received in succession. This Yoga has decayed here by great lapse of time, O queller of foes.

3. I have this day declared that same ancient Yoga to thee; (for) thou art My devotee and comrade, and this secret is indeed the highest.

4. Arjuna said: Later Thy birth, earlier Vivaswan's birth. How am I to understand Thou wert the first to teach?

5. The Glorious Lord said: Many

births of Mine and also of thine are past, O Arjuna. I know them all, (but) thou knowest (them) not, O queller of foes.

6. Though unborn, though the immutable Lord of creatures, yet resting on nature that is Mine I can come into birth by My Creative Power.

7. Whenever there is deterioration of virtue and the predominance of vice, O Bharata, then I bring forth Myself.

8. For the salvation of the good, for the destruction of evil-doers, for the sake of affirming virtue, I take birth age after age.

9. He who really understands My birth and action divine, he, leaving the body, comes not to re-birth, comes unto Me, O Arjuna.

10. Divested of desire, fear and anger, full of Me, sheltered in Me, many

purified by knowledge and austerity have attained to My nature.

11. Howsoever men supplicate Me, even so do I serve them. From every side, O Partha, men tread the path unto Me.

12. Seekers of (direct) success of actions here sacrifice to the gods. Indeed action-born success is quick in the world of men.

13. The fourfold race-colour was created by Me through the distribution of attributes and functions. Though I am the author thereof, do thou know Me as (if I were) an immutable non-actor.

14. Actions do not soil Me; (for) in Me there is no desire for action-fruit. He, who seeks to know Me thus, is not fettered by actions.

15. Action was performed even by

former liberation-seekers, thus informed. Therefore do thou, also, perform action, (as) formerly performed by the ancients.

16. "What is action? What is inaction?" In this even the learned are perplexed. I will declare to thee that action, knowing which thou shalt be rid of evil.

17. But then action must be understood, also misaction must be understood and inaction must be understood. The course of action is intricate.

18. He who sees inaction in action and action in inaction, he among men is intelligent. He is a Yoga-settled, perfect actor.

19. He whose undertakings are all detached from the fancies of desire,

whose actions are (thus) consumed by the fire of wisdom, him the wise call a *pandita*.

20. Renouncing attachment to action and fruit, always satisfied, dependent on nothing, he really does nothing, even when impelled to action.

21. Inexpcetant, subdued in mind and body, averse to gains, he, by performing merely bodily acts, incurs no sin.

22. Satisfied with unsought gain, surmounting the duals, envyless, equable in success and failure, he, even though acting, does not fetter himself.

23. Of one, whose attachment is gone, who is (thus) free, whose mind rests on wisdom, the action performed for the sake of sacrifice is completely dissolved.

24. Brahma is the act of offering. Brahma pours Brahma-oblation into Brahma-fire. Brahma is, indeed, the goal of one thus affixed to Brahma-action.

25. Some Yogis offer sacrifice to the gods. Some pour (this) sacrifice into Brahma-fire by sacrifice itself.

26. Some pour the senses, beginning with the sense of hearing, into the fire of restraint. Some pour sense-objects, beginning with sound, into sense-fires.

27. Some pour all sense-functions and vital functions into the wisdom-lit fire of self control.

28. Likewise some ascetics with steadfast vows are sacrificers with wealth, sacrificers with austerity, sacrificers with Yoga, and sacrificers with the knowledge derived from good reading.

29. Some whose highest aim is the regulation of the vital currents, stopping the course of the incoming and outgoing currents, pour the incoming current into the outgoing current and likewise the outgoing current into the incoming current. Some regulated in food pour the vital currents into the vital currents.

30. These sacrifice-knowers, even all, are destroyers of sin by sacrifice, and tasting the *amrita* at the completion of sacrifice go to Brahma Eternal.

31. Even this world is not for the non-sacrificer. How then the other, O best of the Kurus.

32. Thus sacrifices of many varieties are spread out at the mouth of Brahma. Know they are action-born. Thus knowing, unfetter thyself.

33. Wisdom-sacrifice is, O queller of

foes, better than wealth-constituted sacrifice. Every perfect action, O Partha, concludes in wisdom.

34. Do thou learn it by homage, by questioning and by service. The wise truth-discerners will teach thee the wisdom.

35. Knowing which thou shalt not again thus fall into confusion, O Pandava; and by it thou wilt see all creatures, without exception, in the self, then in Me.

36. Even though of all sinners thou be the most sin-committing, thou shalt pass across all sin with the raft of (this) wisdom alone.

37. As well-lit fire reduces fuel to ashes, O Arjuna, so wisdom-fire reduces all action to ashes.

38. Indeed, as a purifier there is not

here the like of wisdom. The Yoga-perfected one without other's help finds it in the self in time.

39. One, endued with faith, gains wisdom if he is diligent and controls his senses. Having gained wisdom he in no time obtains supreme peace.

40. Ignorant and wanting in faith, the doubter perishes. Neither this world, nor the here-after, nor happiness, is for the doubter.

41. Actions, O Dhananjaya, bind not him whose actions are surrendered to Yoga, whose doubts are cut away by wisdom, and who is self-possessed.

42. Therefore cutting asunder this thine ignorance-born, heart-seated doubt with the sword of wisdom, be thou settled in Yoga. Stand up, O Bharata.

Thus, in the Upanishad of the Glorious Divine Lay, the Science of Brahma, the Ordinance of Yoga, the Discourse between the Glorious Krishna and Arjuna, the Fourth Chapter entitled "The Wisdom Yoga."

THE WISDOM YOGA

CHAPTER V

Surrender of Action

Arjuna said: O Krishna, Thou commendest Sannyasa of actions, and again Thou commendest Yoga. Tell me decisively which is the better of these two.

2. The Glorious Lord said: Both Sannyasa and action-Yoga are infallible producers of good; but of the two, the Yoga of action is preferable to the Sannyasa of action.

3. Be it known that he is a constant Sannyasi who neither dislikes nor desires; for O mighty-armed, one unaffected by the duals easily releases himself from bondage.

4. It is boys who say "Sankhya and Yoga are diverse," not the *panditas*.

One, fully established in either, finds the (common) fruit of both.

5. The position, which is attained by the Sankhyas, is reached by the Yogis also. He sees who sees Sankhya and Yoga as one.

6. But, O mighty-armed, Yogaless Sannyasa is to get misery. The Yoga-endued *muni* attains to Brahma in no time.

7. He who is Yoga-endued, whose self is thoroughly purified, whose self is fully subdued, whose self is become the self of every creature, he, even though acting, is untainted.

8. "Not even anything do I" should the Yoga-endued truth-discerner think in seeing, hearing, touching, smelling, eating, walking, sleeping, breathing,

9. Speaking, discharging, seizing, and

even in eyelid-opening and eyelid-closing, holding that senses are moving amid sense-objects.

10. He who, reposing actions in Brahma, acts renouncing attachment, is unsoiled by sin as the lotus-leaf by water.

11. With the body, with the will, with the understanding, even with the simple senses, Yogis, renouncing attachment, perform action for self-purification.

12. The Yoga-fixed one, renouncing the fruit of action, attains to settled peace. One unendued with Yoga, being attached to fruit by the action of desire, becomes fettered.

13. Resigning all actions by the will, like a victor, the Embodied One rests at ease in the nine-gated house, neither acting nor causing to act.

14. The Lord creates not the agency or actions of men, nor the union of action and fruit; but Nature exerts.

15. The Manifold Being receives neither the sin of any one, nor even the good done by him. Wisdom is enveloped by unwisdom, by which those that come into birth become bewildered.

16. But those in whom the unwisdom of the self is destroyed by wisdom, in them wisdom like the sun discovers That, the Supreme.

17. Those who fix in That the understanding, in That the self, in That the faith, in That the goal, they, being completely washed of their sins by wisdom, reach whence there is no fall.

18. Panditas are those who see the "equal" in a Brahmana possessed of learning and humility, in a cow, in

an elephant, and even in a dog and a dog-eater.

19. Even here is birth conquered by those whose minds are grounded in equality. Indeed, the spotless Brahma is (every where) equal; in that Brahma they are fixed.

20. One should not exult on getting the agreeable, nor be vexed on getting the disagree-able: the knower of Brahma being of settled mind and unconfounded becomes established in Brahma.

21. Unattached to external contacts, he finds the joy that is in the self. Settled in communion with Brahma, he tastes joy undecaying.

22. Those, however, that are contact-born enjoyments, having a beginning and an ending, are, indeed, wombs of

misery. The wise man, O son of Kunti, delights not therein.

23. He who, before release from the body, can here stand the wave springing from desire and wrath, that man is Yoga-fixed, that man is happy.

24. He who is happy within, who is at ease within, who also is radiant within, that Yogi, Brahma-natured, attains to extinguishment in Brahma.

25. Those sages find extinguishment in Brahma, whose sins are destroyed, whose doubts are cut away, whose self is controlled and who are intent upon the welfare of all creatures.

26. To the self-knowers, completely liberated from desire and wrath, subdued in conduct, subdued in mind, extinguishment in Brahma comes quickly.

27. Expelling external contacts,

fixing the eye betwixt the eye brows, equalizing the incoming and outgoing currents which pass through the nostrils,

28. Controlling the senses, the will, and the understanding, the meditator is intent upon liberation as his goal. Ever free, indeed, is he whose desire, fear, and wrath have completely passed away.

29. (Then) knowing Me as the Taster of sacrifices and austerities, as the Highest Lord of all the worlds, as the Lover of every creature, he finds peace.

Thus, in the Upanishad of the Glorious Divine lay, the Science of Brahma, the Ordinance of Yoga, the Discourse between the Glorious Krishna and Arjuna, the Fifth Chapter entitled "The Yoga of Surrender of Action."

CHAPTER VI

Meditation

The Glorious Lord said: He who, independent of the fruit of action, performs action which ought to be done, he is a Sannyasi and he is a Yogi, not he that merely renounces the sacrificial fire or action.

2. That which is called Sannyasa, do thou know that to be Yoga, O Pandava; for, without renouncing the conception of desire one can never be a Yogi.

3. For a muni climbing up Yoga, action is said to be the means; for him, Yoga-mounted, pacification is said to be the means.

4. When one forms no attachment amidst sense-objects or amidst actions,

he, a renouncer of every fancy of desire, is then said to be Yoga-mounted.

5. The self should raise the self, should not lower the self: for the self is verily the friend of the self, and the self is verily the enemy of the self.

6. The self is the friend of that self by which self the self is conquered; but to one, conquered by the non-self, the self moves in enmity as a foe.

7. The self of the self-conquered and tranquillized becomes settled in the Supreme, amidst heat, cold, pleasure and pain, also amidst honour and dishonour.

8. The Yogi whose self is satisfied with the discrimination of reason, who is settled in principle, whose senses are completely subdued, is called Yoga-settled, to whom a lump of earth, a

stone, and gold are the same.

9. He who has equanimity amidst lover, friend, foe, the high-seated, the neutral, the hateful and relatives, amidst the virtuous and even amidst the vicious, he excels.

10. The Yogi should always harmonise himself, living in retirement, alone, having the mind and the self under control, unexpectant and uncovetous.

11. Firmly fixing on a clean spot for himself a seat, neither too high nor too low, of cloth, deer skin and grass, arranged one over another,

12. There placing himself on the seat, making the will single-pointed, with feeling and sense functions under control, he should practise Yoga for the purification of the self.

13. Evenly holding the body, head, and neck, unmoved and steady, gazing on the tip of his nose without looking in (other) directions,

14. Being self-serene, fearless, adopting the discipline of a Vedic student, controlling the will, directing his feeling towards Me, the Yogi should sit aiming at Me as the highest goal.

15. Thus constantly fixing the self, the Yogi, regulated in mind, obtains the peace which culminates in extinguishment, and abides in Me.

16. But Yoga is not for him who eats too much, nor again for him who eats not the least; nor for him who is very sleepy or even wakeful, O Arjuna.

17. To one, regular in food and diversions, regular in efforts amid actions, regular in sleep and

wakefulness, Yoga becomes a destroyer of misery.

18. When his mind, thoroughly regulated, rests solely on the self, then, becoming unsolicitous of every desire, he is said to be a perfected Yogi.

19. "As a lamp in a windless place flickers not," such is the simile imagined of the Yogi of concentrated attention, absorbed in communion with the self.

20. That in which his mind controlled by Yoga-practice becomes tranquil; that in which seeing the self by the self he is satisfied in the self,

21. And experiences the boundless supersensuous pleasure, apprehensible by the understanding; and that, in which established, he moves not from the reality,

22. And gaining which, he thinks no other gain greater than it, and being established in it is not ruffled by even heavy affliction;

23. That immunity from the accession of pain should be known as what is called Yoga. This Yoga should be held fast with a resolute mind.

24. Rejecting with a will all fancy-born desires, without exception, also regulating the sense-group all round,

25. Step by step, one should abstain, and fixing the mind on the self by constancy-grasped understanding, should not think of anything (else).

26. Whithersoever may the mind, volatile and unsteady, wander forth, therefrom he should, ruling it, restore it in subjection to the self.

27. For, to such tranquil-minded,

passion-pacified, Brahma-natured and sinless Yogi, comes the highest bliss.

28. (It is) thus by constantly engaging the self that the Yogi entirely freed from sin, easily tastes the boundless happiness of contact with Brahma.

29. One whose self is settled in Yoga, having an equal eye for all, sees the self abiding in all creatures and all creatures in the self.

30. He who sees Me in all, and sees all in Me, I am not lost to him, nor is he lost to Me.

31. He who settled on the Oneness serves Me as abiding in all creatures, that Yogi moving through every circumstance moves in Me.

32. He who sees the pleasure or the pain in every creature the same as his own by comparison, he is the Yogi held

supreme, O Arjuna.

33. Arjuna said: Of this Yoga through equalization, that Thou hast declared, O Madhusudana, I see no stable basis on account of (our natural) fickleness.

34. For, O Krishna, the mind is restless, violent, powerful and stubborn. The control of it like that of the wind is, I think, very difficult to effect.

35. The Glorious Lord said: No doubt, O mighty-armed, the mind is difficult of control and restless. But practice and dispassionateness, O son of Kunti, do control it.

36. Yoga, I think, is hardly attainable by one, whose self is uncontrolled; but it can be attained with method by the self-controlled and assiduous.

37. Arjuna said: When one, endued with faith, has not subdued himself, and

his mind has fallen off from Yoga before attaining to Yoga-perfection, what course does he tread, O Krishna?

38. Fallen off from both, does he not perish like a rent cloud, O mighty-armed, supportless and bewildered in the path of Brahma?

39. O Krishna, Thou art able to cut away this my doubt completely. Any other than Thyself to cut away this doubt, is not to be found.

40. The Glorious Lord said: Ruin is not for him, O Partha, either here or hereafter; for, brother, a doer of good never walks a path of misery.

41. Obtaining the worlds of meritorious workers and dwelling therein for countless years, he who fell from Yoga finds birth in the house of the pure and glorious.

42. Or may find birth even in the family of intelligent Yogis: birth such as this is, indeed, very hard to get in this world.

43. Therein he regains the Yoga of understanding pertaining to his former body, and thence diligently strives again for complete success, O son of the Kurus.

44. For he is certainly driven helpless by that former habit. Even the mere enquirer about Yoga transcends the Word-Brahma.

45. Thus striving with assiduity the Yogi, completely freed from sin, fully perfected through many births, then passes on to the highest goal.

46. The Yogi is greater than the ascetics; he is thought greater than even men of knowledge. The Yogi is greater

than the men of action. Therefore, O Arjuna, be a Yogi.

47. Of all Yogis again, he who with the inner self abiding in Me, full of faith serves Me, he, I think, is the most completely settled.

Thus, in the Upanishad of the Glorious Divine Lay, the Science of Brahma, the Ordinance of Yoga, the Discourse between the Glorious Krishna and Arjuna, the Sixth Chapter entitled "The Meditation Yoga."

CHAPTER VII

Discrimination

The Glorious Lord said: Hear, O Partha, how with mind attached to Me, by practising Yoga reliant on Me, thou shalt doubtless know Me to the utmost.

2. I will fully declare to thee this wisdom discriminately, which being known, nothing else again will be left here to be known.

3. Of men, hardly one in a thousand strives for success. Of successful strivers, hardly one knows Me truly.

4. Earth, water, fire, air, ether, will, understanding, egoism: thus eightfold is this My active Nature divided.

5. This is the Inferior. But do thou know My other active Nature, the

Superior, manifested in the creature-soul, whereby this universe is upheld, O mighty-armed.

6. Believe that all creatures are of this womb. I am (the cause of) the manifestation, also the dissolution, of this universe.

7. Superior to Me nothing else is, O Dhananjaya. On me is woven all this like clusters of jewels on a string.

8. I am flavour in waters, O son of Kunti, beaming light in moon and sun, the *pranava* (vital word) in all the Vedas, sound in ether, manliness in men,

9. The pure fragrance in earth, heat in fire, the life in all creatures, and austerity in the ascetics.

10. Know Me, O Partha, as the seed eternal of all creatures. Of the rational I am the understanding; of the energetic

I am the energy,

11. And I the strength of the strong, devoid of the tinge of desire. O mighty Bharata, in creatures I am desire unopposed to right.

12. And those that are good-natured and those that are passionate or dark, are, indeed, from Me. Thus know them to be; but not that I am in them, or they are in Me.

13. Confounded by these susceptibilities formed by the three attributes, the world seeks not to know Me, the Supreme beyond them, the Immutable.

14. This attributeful power, My Maya, is indeed divine, and hard to transcend. It is only those who seek refuge in Me that swim across this Maya.

15. Unto Me come not the

confounded evildoers, the vilest of men, robbed of reason by the Power and sheltered in demoniac nature.

16. Four Kinds of doers of good devote themselves to Me, O Arjuna: the afflicted, the enquiring, the object-seeking, and the wise, O mighty Bharata.

17. Among these is distinguished the wise man, always settled in Yoga and devoted to the One; for above all objects I am dear to the wise man, he too is dear to Me.

18. Noble, indeed, are all these but I hold the wise man is verily the self; for with the self settled in Yoga he seeks refuge solely in Me, the Goal unexcelled.

19. At the end of numerous births he who knows "Vasudeva is all," humbly approaches My feet. Such a noble self is very rare.

20. Robbed of wisdom by various desires, men resort to other gods, adopting their respective observances, led by their respective natures.

21. Whatever the form a devotee wishes to worship with faith, that faith I, indeed, ordain for him.

22. Endued with that faith he strives to worship that form and thence gains the desires, verily by Me allowed.

23. But to these, the little-minded, that fruit becomes finite. The sacrificers to the gods go unto the gods, My devotees come even unto Me.

24. The unintelligent, not knowing My nature supreme, imperishable and unexcelled, think Me the unmanifest as one limited by the manifestation.

25. Nor am I discovered of all, surrounded by the combinative Power.

This world, being deluded, seeks not to know Me, the Unborn, the Imperishable.

26. O Arjuna, I know creatures past, present and to come, but no one knows Me.

27. O Bharata, by the dual delusion arising from desire and aversion, all creatures at birth go to complete bewilderment, O terror of foes.

28. It is those men of meritorious deeds whose sin has come to an end, that, freed from the dual delusion, devote themselves to Me with strenuous vows.

29. They who for liberation from infirmity and death strive reliant on Me; they know That Brahma, all-presiding Self, and the all-compassing Act. (Tat Brahma, Kritsna Adhyatma, Akhila Karma).

30. And they who know Me as Lord of creature-nature and spirit-nature (adhibhuta, adhidaiva) and as Lord of sacrifice (adhiyajna), they in a Yoga-settled mind know Me even at the time of their death.

Thus, in the Upanishad of the Glorious Divine Lay, the Science of Brahma, the Ordinance of Yoga, the Discourse between the Glorious Krishna and Arjuna, the Seventh Chapter entitled "The Yoga of Discriminate Wisdom."

CHAPTER VIII
The Redeeming Brahma

Arjuna said: What is That Brahma, what Adhyatma, what Karma, O Being Most High? And what is declared Adhibhuta and what is called Adhidaiva?

2. How and who here in this body is Adhiyajna, O Madhusudana? And how to those who are of regulated selves dost Thou become knowable at the time of their death?

3. The Glorious Lord said: The Immutable is the Supreme Brahma, (whose) own (inner) nature is called the Paramount Self (Adhyatma), (whose) varied evolution of creature-natures is named *(Akhila) Karma*.

4. *Adhibhuta* is the nature productive of changes (or phenomena), and *Adhidaivata* is the Presiding Spirit. Here in this body I am *Adhiyajna* (Lord of sacrifice), O best of bodyholders (man).

5. And he attains to My nature who remembering Me in his last moments departs released from the body. In this there is no doubt.

6. Whatsoever the nature one contemplates when leaving the body at the time of death, even that is the nature he gets having been constantly affected by that nature, O son of Kunti.

7. Therefore, at all times earnestly remember Me and fight. Dedicating thy will and understanding to Me thou shalt come unto Me without doubt.

8. One meditating with undeviating mind, settled by means of practice, goes

to the Supreme Presiding Spirit Divine, O Partha.

9. He who earnestly remembers the Omniscient, the Ancient, the All-Ruler, the Atom of atoms, of all the Upholder, of Form unimaginable, shining as the sun beyond the darkness,

10. At the time of death with unwavering will, being helped by devotion and also by Yoga-power, settling the life-current betwixt the eye-brows, he goes to the Supreme Presiding Spirit Divine.

11. That which the Veda-knowers call the Immutable, That which the dispassionate ascetics feel, That, which is the object of those who observe the Vedic students' discipline, That Goal I will compendiously declare to thee.

12. Controlling all the gates,

confining the mind in the heart, settling the life-current in his own head, affirmed in Yoga-constancy,

13. Reciting 'Om,' the One Imperishable Brahma so called, earnestly remembering Me, he who departs leaving the body reaches the Supreme Goal.

14. He who with undeviating mind always remembers Me from day to day, to him, the Yogi in constant communion, I am easily accessible, O Partha.

15. The Great-souled, having attained to Me, having (therefore) attained the highest perfection, get no rebirth, the abode of misery, the impermanent.

16. The worlds from Brahma's world (down to this) are revolutionary; but reaching Me, O son of Kunti, there is

no rebirth known.

17. Those who know Brahma's day completed in a thousand cycles and (his) night completed in a thousand cycles are men cognizant of Day and Night.

18. From the Unmanifested come forth all manifestations at the approach of Day. At the approach of Night they dissolve in what is called the Unmanifested.

19. This very group of creatures, appearing again and again, dissolve at the approach of Night. Powerless, O Partha, it streams forth at the coming of Day.

20. But higher than that Unmanifested is another Unmanifested Being Eternal, that perishes not while all creatures die.

21. The Unmanifested, thus declared as Imperishable, is That called the

Supreme Goal, attaining to which none
return. That supreme position is Mine.

22. But that Supreme Presiding Spirit,
O Partha, in whom creatures are
abiding, by whom all this is pervaded,
is accessible by devotion that
is underviating.

23. That time when departed Yogis
find non-return or return, that time I will
declare, O mighty Bharata.

24. Fire (which is) light, day time, the
light fortnight, the six-monthy
northward course,—then departed
Brahma-knowing men go to Brahma.

25. Smoke, night time, the dark
fortnight, the six-monthly southward
course,—then the Yogi obtaining lunar
light returns.

26. The Light and the Dark: these are
held to be the eternal paths of the

universe. By the one he obtains non-return, by the other returns.

27. The Yogi, O Partha, becoming cognizant of these paths is not bewildered. Therefore, at all times, be linked to Yoga, O Arjuna.

18. In the Vedas, in sacrifices, in austerities and also in alms-givings whatever fruit of merit is declared, the Yogi having known this passes beyond all that, and attains to the Supreme Seat Original.

Thus, in the Upanishad of the Glorious Divine Lay, the Science of Brahma, the Ordinance of Yoga, the Discourse between the Glorious Krishna and Arjuna, the Eighth Chapter entitled "The Yoga of the Indestructible (Redeeming) Brahma.

CHAPTER IX

The Sovereign Mystery

The Glorious Lord said: Now to thee, the uncavilling, I will declare the most secret wisdom together with discriminate wisdom, knowing which thou shalt free thyself from evil.

2. The sovereign science, the sovereign mystery is this, holy, the highest, directly felt, righteous, very easy to perform and undiminishing.

3. Men having no faith in this piety, O terror of foes, without reaching Me, roll back into the paths of the world of death.

4. All this world is pervaded by Me in unmanifest forms. All creatures depend on Me but I depend not on them.

5. Nor again do creatures depend on Me. Behold My divine power of combination: sustainer of creatures but aloof from creatures is My Self, the creator of creatures.

6. As ever placed in ether is the vast air that goes everywhere, so placed in Me are all creatures. Thus imagine.

7. All creatures, O son of Kunti, revert into My nature at the expiration of the decreed term. Again at the beginning of a decreed term I variously send them forth.

8. Abiding in My own active nature, again and again I variously send forth this entire creature-group, powerless under Nature's sway.

9. But these acts, O Dhananjaya, bind not Me, seated, as if, on high, dissociated from those acts.

10. I presiding, Nature brings forth the universe of mobiles and immobiles. For this reason, O son of Kunti, the universe rolls on.

11. Without knowing My supreme nature as great Lord of creatures, the confounded disregard Me in human form,

12. (They being) with hopes in vain, with deeds in vain, with wisdom in vain, wrong-minded and sheltered in delusive nature, greedy and demoniac.

13. But the high-souled, O Partha, sheltered in godly nature devote themselves to Me with undeviating will, knowing Me as the Inexhaustible source of creatures.

14. Those that are settled in Yoga adore Me with devotion, always preaching Me, persevering firm in vow

and bowing down to Me.

15. Others again sacrificing with wisdom-sacrifice adore Me as the Unity whose face is the universe varied and multiple.

16. I the Vedic sacrifice, I the *Smarta* sacrifice, I the ancestral offering, I the cereals, I the formula, even the butter I, fire I, the burnt offering I.

17. I the father, mother, supporter and grandsire of the universe, (I) the object of knowledge, the holy "Om," the Rik, Sama and Yajus.

18. The goal, nourisher, lord, spectator, the abode, the shelter, lover, manifester, dissolver, the resting place, the nursery, the seed unperishing.

19. I give heat. I withhold and discharge rain. I am immortality and also death, the real and the unreal

(phenomenal), O Arjuna.

20. Men of the Triple Science, soma-drinkers freed from sin, worshipping Me by sacrifice seek the heaven of gratification. Repairing to the pure world of the Chief of the gods they taste the excellent enjoyments of the gods in heaven.

21. Having enjoyed the spacious heaven-world they return to the mortal world on the exhaustion of their merit. Thus relying on the rites of the Triple, desire-seekers have the reward of going forward and backward.

22. For those men who adore meditating on Me without deviation, for them thus constantly settled in Yoga, I carry the burden of supply and protection.

23. Even those devotees who sacrifice

to other gods with faith, even they, O son of Kunti, sacrifice, indeed, to Me, contrary to rule.

24. For, of all sacrifices I am the taster and the Lord; but seek not to know Me in truth, hence fall off.

25. Votaries of the gods go unto the gods, to the ancestors go ancestor-votaries, to the creatures go the sacrificers to creatures, the sacrificers to Me come even unto Me.

26. A leaf, a flower, a fruit, water, whatever one offers Me with devoutness, that offering of love I accept of the self-controlled.

27. Whatsoever thou performest, whatsoever eatest, whatsoever sacrificest, whatsoever givest away, whatever austerity performest, O son of Kunti, dedicate it to Me.

28. Thus from the action-bonds of good and evil fruit thou shalt be released. With the self allied to Sannyasa and Yoga thou shalt, completely freed, come unto Me.

29. Alike am I amid all creatures. None is hateful or dear to me. But they who serve Me with devotion, they are in Me, and even in them am I.

30. If one, even most ill-behaved, serves Me with undeviating devotion he should be thought good indeed; for he is rightly cognizant;

31. Speedily becomes righteous-souled and goes to ever-lasting peace. O son of Kunti, avow "My devotee never perishes."

32. Relying on Me, O Partha, whoever they may be, even though of sinful womb, women, Vaishyas

likewise Shudras, even they reach the Supreme Goal.

33. How much more then the holy Brahmanas and devout royal sages! Coming into this impermanent world (so) full of evil, do thou devote thyself to Me.

34. Fix thy mind on Me, be My devotee, sacrifice to Me, bow down to Me. Thus disposing the self and fixing thy supreme goal in Me thou shalt come to Me indeed.

Thus, in the Upanishad of the Glorious Divine Lay, the Science of Brahma, the Ordinance of Yoga, the Discourse between the Glorious Krishna and Arjuna, the Ninth Chapter entitled "The Sovereign Secret-Yoga."

CHAPTER X

Divine Diversifications

The Glorious Lord said: Listen again, O mighty-armed, to My supreme word, which I will declare to thee so heartily interested, from a desire for thy good.

2. Neither the gods nor the great saints know (all) My manifestations, for, in every respect, I an the origin of the gods and great saints.

3. He who knows Me as the Unborn, Beginningless, Supreme Lord of the universe, he, the unerring among mortals, is freed from all sins.

4. Understanding, perception, unconfoundedness, forgiveness, truthfulness, dispassionateness, tranquillity, pleasure, pain, energy, abnegation, fear

and also fearlessness,

5. Harmlessness, equanimity, content, austerity, charity, approbation and disapprobation are (good) characteristics of creatures, derived, indeed, from Me.

6. The seven great sages, the prior four, also the Manus, deriving characteristics from Me, sprung from My Will, were those whose issue are these (now) in the world.

7. Whoever really understands this My diversification and combination, unhesitatingly adopts Yoga. In this there is no doubt.

8. I am the manifester of all, all evolves from Me. Thus thinking, the wise, endowed with their characteristics, devote themselves to Me.

9. Those whose minds are devoted to

Me, whose vital currents are centred in Me, find comfort and delight in instructing one another and constantly preaching Me.

10. To these, thus in constant communion and hearty devotion, I give the aid of that understanding whereby they come unto Me.

11. Indeed, for the sake of compassion for them, I, seated in their characteristics, destroy the ignorance-born darkness by the shining lamp of wisdom.

12. Arjuna said: Supreme Brahma, Supreme Abode, Supreme Holiness art Thou. The Divine Presiding Being everlasting, the Primeval God, the Unborn, the Manifold Being,

13. All saints call Thee. So also do the godly saint Narada, Asita, Devala

and Vyasa, and Thyself also tellest me so.

14. All this that Thou sayest to me, I hold to be true, O Keshava. Thy manifestation, O Lord, neither gods nor demons know.

15. Thou alone knowest the self by the self, O Being most High, creator of creatures, Lord of creatures, God of gods, Governor of the universe.

16. Thou canst, without reserve, tell me what are the conspicuous self-diversifications, by which diversifications pervading these worlds Thou abidest.

17. How, O Yogin, may I constantly meditating know Thee? And in what and what beings art Thou the object of my contemplation, O Lord.

18. Tell me again by amplification the

combination and diversification of the Self, O Janardana; for, there is no satiety for me in hearing of the Immortal.

19. The Glorious Lord said: Blessing on thee! I will declare to thee what are the conspicuous diversifications of the Self throught the chief ones. There is no limit, O best of the Kurus, to My expansion.

20. O Gudakesha, I am the self seated in the heart of every creature. I am the beginning, the middle and also the end of all creatures.

21. I am Vishnu among the Adityas, the beaming sun among lights, Marichi among the Maruts, the moon among the stars of night,

22. The Sama-veda among the Vedas, Vasava among the gods, the mind among the faculties, consciousness

among creatures,

23. Shankara among the Rudras, the Lord of riches among the Yakshas and Rakshasas, the Purifier (Fire) among the Vasus, Meru among the peaked (mountains).

24. Also know Me, O Partha, as Vrihaspati, the chief of household priests, I am Skanda among generals, the ocean among reservoirs of water,

25. Bhrigu among the great saints, the one-lettered among words, the recital-sacrifice among the sacrifices, the Himalaya among the immovables.

26. The Ashwattha among all trees, Narada among the godly saints, Chitraratha among the Gandharvas, Kapila the muni among the perfected.

27. Know Me as the amrita-sprung erect-eared among the horses, Airavata

among the elephant-chiefs, and the ruler of men among men.

28. I am the thunderbolt among offensive weapons, the desire-milker among cows, and I the progenitor Kandarpa, I am Vasuki among the hooded snakes,

29. Ananta among the unhooded snakes, Varuna among the water inhabitants, Yama among the rulers,

30. Prahlada among the Daityas, Time among the reckoners, the lion among the beasts, Vainateya among the birds,

31. The wind among the fast-going, Rama among the armed men, the crocodile among the fishes, the Jahnavi among the streams.

32. I am the beginning and the termination and also the middle of creatures, O Arjuna. I am the Adhyatma

science among the sciences, and I am the true proposition of logicians.

33. Of letters I am "A," and of composite words, the dwandwa. I, also, am inexhaustible time, I the supporter universe-faced.

34. And I am all-absorbing death, and the rise of all that are to be. And in women I am fame, prosperity, (good) speech, memory, intelligence, constancy and forgiveness.

35. I am also the Vrihat-sama of the Samas, and the Gayatri among the metres. I am the Margashirsha among the months, and the flowering spring among the seasons.

36. I am dice of the cheats, the radiance of the radiant. I am victory, I am true knowledge, I am goodness in the good.

37. I am Vasudeva among the Vrishnis, Dhananjaya among the Pandavas, also Vyasa among the munis, the sage Ushana among the expounders.

38. I am the sceptre of governors, the policy of victors, the reticence of silent workers, and the reason of the rational.

39. And, O Arjuna, I am that which is the seed of all creatures. There is no creature, moving or unmoving, that exists without Me.

40. O terror of foes, there is no end to My glorious diversifications, and this expansion of diversifications has been only indicatively declared by Me.

41. Whatever entity is singular, glorious or energetic, do thou know that to have sprung from fragments of My Splendour.

42. But what is it to thee by this

manifold knowing, O Arjuna? Pervading this whole universe with a part of Myself I am staying.

Thus in the Upanishad of the Glorious Divine Lay, the Science of Brahma, the Ordinance of Yoga, the Discourse between the Glorious Krishna and Arjuna, the Tenth Chapter entitled "The Yoga of Divine Diversifications."

CHAPTER XI

The Vision of the Universal Form

Arjuna said: This my confoundedness has been dispelled by that word, the Adhyatmanamed, the Supreme Secret, which Thou hast declared to favour me.

2. I have heard in detail from Thee, O Lotus-leaf-eyed, of the manifestation and dissolution of creatures, and even of the High Selfhood imperishable.

3. Even so is This as Thou declarest the Self, O Lord Supreme. (But) I feel a curiosity to see Thy Lordly Form, O Being Most High.

4. Shouldst Thou, O Lord, think I could see it, then, O Master of Combination, show Thou the Imperishable Self to me.

5. The Glorious Lord said: Behold, O Partha, My forms by hundreds and by thousands, various in kind, glorious, various in colour and shape.

6. Behold the Adityas, the Vasus, the Rudras, the twin Ashwins, likewise the Maruts. Behold many marvels unseen before, O Bharata.

7. Behold to-day, in My body, O Gudakesha, all the world of the moving and unmoving together and anything else thou desirest to see.

8. But with these thine eyes thou wilt not be able to see Me. I give thee the celestial eye: Behold My masterly combination.

9. Sanjaya said: O King, Hari, the great master of combination, thus saying then showed Partha the Supreme Lordly form,

10. With many mouths and eyes, with many wonderful sights, with splendid ornaments, with many uplifted shining weapons,

11. Bearing splendid garlands and dresses, anointed with celestial fragrances, all-marvellous, luminous, boundless, universe-faced.

12. If the splendour of a thousand suns were to appear together on the sky, it would be a semblance of the splendour of that Great Self.

13. There the Pandava then saw together the whole universe, divided manifold, in the body of the god of gods.

14. Then he, Dhananjaya, overwhelmed with astonishment, with his hair standing on end, bowing with his head, with joined palms addressed the god.

15. Arjuna said: In Thy body, O God, I see all the celestials, likewise distinct creature-groups, the Lord Brahma on his lotus-seat, all the saints and celestial crawlers.

16. I everywhere see Thee, possessed of numerous arms, bellies, mouths and eyes, in form unbounded. I find no end, no middle nor again Thy beginning, O Lord of the Universe, O Form Universal.

17. Diademed, sceptred, discus-in-hand, Thee the Immense do I behold, a mass of splendour, illuminating all and dazzling the gaze like the blazing fire and the sun.

18. Thou the Immutable, the Supreme, the object to be known, Thou the First Nursery of the Universe. Thou the Unperishing Guardian of Eternal

Virtue, Thou art the Immemorial Presiding Being, think I.

19. I find Thee without beginning, middle and end, unlimited in power, possessing numberless arms, having the Moon and Sun for Thine eyes, and the blazing fire for Thy mouth, heating the Universe with Thy splendour.

20. This interspace betwixt the Earth and the heavens and all the sides are filled by Thee alone. The triple world is pained at the sight of this Thy stern marvellous form, O Great Self.

21. Those bands of the celestials enter into Thee. Some terrified sing praises with joined palms. Bands of perfected saints saying "all hail" pray to Thee in expressive hymns.

22. The Rudras and Adityas, the Vasus, those that are the Sadhyas, the

Vishwas, the twin Ashwins, the Maruts, the heat drinkers, bands of Gandharvas, Yakshas, celestials and the perfected, all wondering gaze at Thee.

23. Seeing Thy grand form, possessed of many mouths and eyes, many arms, thighs and feet, many breasts and terrible teeth, O mighty-armed, the worlds are troubled, so also am I.

24. For, seeing Thee sky-reaching, blazing, many-coloured, with gaping mouth and blazing eyes wide open, I, troubled in the inner self, lose firmness and comfort, O Vishnu.

25. Also seeing Thy mouths with terrible teeth like Time's insatiable flame, I perceive not the directions nor find I ease. Have mercy, O Lord of the Gods, O Home of the Universe.

26. Into Thee and these sons of

Dhritarashra with numbers of the rulers of the Earth, Bhishma, Drona, likewise that son of Suta, together with our chief warriors,

27. Into Thy terrible mouths with terrible teeth, hurrying enter. Some caught in the interstices of Thy teeth are seen with their best limbs crushed.

28. As the manifold water-currents of rivers flow forward into the ocean, so these heroes of the world of men enter into Thy mouths blazing on all sides.

29. As moths with quickened speed rush into a blazing fire to die, even so to die are men also rushing into Thy mouths with quickened speed.

30. Thou lickest wholly to devour all mankind with flaming mouths. Filling the whole universe with radiance Thy scorching rays are scattering heat

around, O Vishnu.

31. Tell me who Thou art of form severe. I bow to Thee. Have mercy, O God Supreme. I desire to understand Thee, the Primeval One. I comprehend not Thy motive.

32. The Glorious Lord said: I am Time, depopulating, matured, now engaged in gathering in people. Even without being intended by thee, all the warriors, stationed in opposing armies, shall cease to be.

33. Therefore, stand thou up. Win renown. Conquering the foe enjoy prosperous sovereignty. Indeed, these have already been slain by Me. Be thou the ostensible instrument, O left-handed one.

34. Drona and Bhishma and Jayadrath and Karna, likewise other heroes of the

war, have been slain by Me. Do thou kill. Be not troubled. Fight, thou shalt be the conqueror of opponents in battle.

35. Hearing this speech of Keshava, Kiriti with joined palms trembling and prostrating himself and extremely awed, again in a choked voice humbly addressed Krishna.

36. Arjuna said: Justly, O Hrishikesha, Thy glory delights the world and makes it love (Thee), the Rakshasas to fly frightened to every quarter and all the hosts of the perfected to make obeisance.

37. Wherefore, O Great Self, should they not bow to Thee (who art) greater even than Brahma, and art his Original Cause, O Infinite, God of gods, Home of the Universe? Thou art the Imperishable, the Real, the Unreal, That

which is the Supreme.

38. Thou the Primal God, the Presiding Being most ancient. Thou of this universe the last resting-place. Thou the Knower, the Object to be known, and the Supreme Abode. The universe is pervaded by Thee, O Infinite Form.

39. Thou art Vayu, Yama, Agni, Varuna, moon, the Lord of creatures, and primal ancestor. Salutation to Thee a thousand times, again and again salutation to Thee.

40. Salutation before, also behind Thee; salutation to Thee on every side, O All. Of immeasurable strength and unbounded power art Thou. Thou compassest all. Therefore Thou art All.

41. Thinking (Thee) a comrade, not knowing this Thy Majesty, whatever under a mistake or from intimacy I may

have familiarly uttered (as) "O Krishna," "O Yadava," "O comrade,"

42. And whatever irreverence for the sake of jesting, Thou, O Unfallen One, hast received at play, repose, sitting, and meals, alone or in company, the same to forgive I implore Thee, the Immeasurable.

43. Father of this world, of the moving and the unmoving, and adorable more than the preceptor, Thou art. There is none equal to Thee. Where is Thy greater in the triple world, O Thou of incomparable power?

44. Therefore, laying my body prostrate, for Thy grace I move Thee, the Lord adorable. As father with son, as friend with friend, as the beloved with his beloved, bear Thou with me, O God.

45. I have the pleasure of seeing what was never seen before, yet my mind is troubled with fear. O God, show me that other form. Be gracious, O God of gods, Home of the universe.

46. I desire to see Thee, as before, diademed, sceptred, and discus-in-hand. Appear again in that four-sustaining form, O Thou of a thousand arms, O Form Universal.

47. The Glorious Lord said: By Me, gracious through thy communion with the Self, has been revealed this My form, supreme, radiant, universal, infinite, and original, which none, except thyself, has seen before.

48. Neither by Veda, sacrifice and study, nor by almsgiving, nor by deeds, nor by severe austerities can I be seen in this form in the world of men by any

other than thyself, O hero of the Kurus.

49. May thou be without a sense of trouble or confusion at seeing this My stern form. Be terror-freed and glad-hearted. Behold again this My other form.

50. Sanjaya said: Vasudeva addressing Arjuna showed His own form, and the Great Self resuming His amiable shape comforted this terrified one.

51. Arjuna said: Seeing this Thy gentle human form, O Janardana, I am now restored to my faculties, consciousness and nature.

52. The Glorious Lord said: Very difficult to see in this My form, of which thou art the beholder. The gods even are always anxious to have a sight of this form.

53. Neither through the Vedas, nor through austerity, nor through almsgiving, nor through sacrifice can I be seen as thou hast seen Me.

54. But it is by undeviating devotion, O Arjuna, that I can thus be truly known, seen, and felt, O terror of foes.

55. He who acts for Me, who esteems Me as the supreme goal, who is devoted to Me, who has cast off (other) attachment, who is without enmity to any creature, he comes unto Me, O Pandava.

Thus, in the Upanishad of the Glorious Divine Lay, the Science of Brahma, the Ordinance of Yoga, the Discourse between the Glorious Krishna and Arjuna, the Eleventh chapter entitled "The Yoga of the Vision of the Universal Form."

CHAPTER XII

Devotion

Arjuna said: The devout, who thus constantly settled in Yoga, adore Thee, and those, again that adore the Unmanifested Indestructible: of these which are the better instructed in Yoga?

2. The Glorious Lord said: I hold they are the *most* Yoga-settled, who being constantly settled in Yoga, fixing their attention on Me, adore Me with the highest faith.

3. But those who adore the Indestructible (that is) indefinite, unmanifested, all-pervading, unimaginable, uniform, unchanging and stable,

4. They thoroughly regulating the sense-group, equipoising the under-

standing amid all things, and being intent upon the welfare of all creatures,
also attain to Me.

5. Greater is the trouble of those
whose feelings incline towards the
Unmanifest, for the unmanifest course
is for body-holders hard to pursue.

6. But those who surrendering all
actions unto Me, regarding Me supreme,
meditating on Me, adore (Me) with
undeviating Yoga,

7. Of such whose feelings are settled
on Me I become speedily the deliverer,
O Partha, from the ocean of death
currents.

8. Fix thy will on Me, introduce thy
understanding into Me, thou shalt then
hereafter abide in Me without doubt.

10. If, even to (that) practice thou art
unequal, let actions for Me be thy

highest aim. Even performing action for My sake thou shalt attain to success.

11. If even this thou hast not the strength to do, then resigned unto Me and self-controlled, renounce the fruit of all actions.

12. Perception is certainly better than (blind) practice; reflexion, better than perception; renunciation of action-fruit, better than reflexion; peace, inseparate from renunciation.

13. Not hating any creature, being friendly and also merciful, holding nothing as his own, unegoistic, alike in pleasure and pain, forgiving,

14. Always contented, assiduous in Yoga, self-regulated, firm in principle, with will and understanding surrendered to Me, he that is devoted to Me is dear to Me.

15. He who is not disturbed by the world, who disturbs not the world, who is free from the disturbances of exultation, anger, and fear, he also is dear to Me.

16. Undepending, pure, expert, exalted, untroubled, a renouncer of every undertaking, he that is devoted to me is dear to Me.

17. He who neither exults or hates, nor laments or desires, who is no seeker of good or evil, who is devout, he is dear to Me.

18. The same to friend and foe, likewise in honour and dishonour; alike in cold and heat, pleasure and pain, completely rid of attachment,

19. Alike in censure and praise, reticent, satisfied with anything and everything, homeless, firm in principle

and devout is the man dear to Me.

20. But exceedingly dear to Me are those devotees that, full of faith, esteeming Me supreme, adhere to this unperishing righteousness as declared.

Thus, in the Upanishad of the Glorious Divine Lay, the Science of Brahma, the Ordinance of Yoga, the Discourse between the Glorious Krishna and Arjuna, the Twelfth Chapter entitled "The Yoga of Devotion."

CHAPTER XIII
Nature and Presiding Being

The Glorious Lord said: This body, O son of Kunti, is called the Field; he that knows it is called the Field-knower. Thus say the knowers of That.

2. And also know Me as the Field-knower in all Fields, O Bharata. I hold that is wisdom, which is wisdom about the Field and the Field-knower.

3. What that field, of what character, into what modifiable and whence what is; and who He is and of what powers: hear from Me compendiously of (all) this,

4. Variously sung by sages in varieties of verses and also in Brahma-indicating expressions, full of well -settled reasons.

5. The vast creatures (elements), egoism, understanding and also the unmanifested, the ten and one senses, and the five sense-pastures,

6. Desire, aversion, pleasure, pain, the compound which is the life-receptacle: thus briefly is the Field with modifications described.

7. Pridelessness, unshowiness, harmlessness, forgiveness, straightforwardness, attentions to preceptor, purity, steadfastness, self-control,

8. Dispassionateness amid senseobjects, also non-egoism and reflexion about birth, death, infirmity, sickness, misery, and evil,

9. Non-attachment to, and nonidentifying with, son, wife, home and the rest, constant equanimity amid desirable and undesirable event.

10. And unswerving devotion to Me with unflinching Yoga, the resorting to sequestered spots, disinclination for promiscuous society.

11. Constancy in Adhyatma-wisdom, reflexion about the aim of true wisdom: (all) this is said to be wisdom. That which is otherwise is un-wisdom.

12. I will (now) declare That which is the Object to be known; knowing which one tastes immortality: That, the Beginningless Brahma, culminating in Me, is declared to be neither the Real nor the Unreal (phenomenal).

13. That abides in all with hands and feet, in all with eyes, heads and mouths, in all with ears, in the world enveloping all.

14. Shining through all sense-attributes, entirely distinct from all the

senses; unattached yet supporting all; attributeless yet sustaining attributes;

15. Outside and inside all creatures; also moving and unmoving; indiscriminate from subtlety at hand and far away is That.

16. Undivided, yet as if distributively seated among creatures, that Object to be known is the sustainer of creatures, also (their) absorber and creator.

17. That is the Light of lights, said to be beyond darkness, is wisdom, Object of wisdom and goal of wisdom, and is seated in every one's bosom.

18. Thus the Field, likewise wisdom and the Object of wisdom are briefly stated. It is My devotee that knowing (all) this discriminately attains to My nature.

19. Know both Nature and Presiding Being to be, indeed, beginningless. Also

know variations and attributes to be Nature-born.

·20. Regarding effect and activity of cause, Nature is said to be the source. Regarding susceptibility to pleasure and pain, the Presiding Being is said to be the source.

21. The Presiding Being, seated in Nature, is affected by the Nature-born attributes, by reason of association with the attributes in his births in good and evil wombs.

22. The Spectator and Appraiser, Taster, Sustainer, Great Lord, and even called the Supreme Self, is the Supreme Presiding Being in this body.

23. He who thus knows the Presiding Being and Nature with her attributes, he, even moving in every condition, seeks not birth again.

24. Some see the Self by the self in the self by meditation, others by the Sankhya-Yoga, others by the action-Yoga;

25. While others, not thus informed, adore as they hear from others. Even these, whose highest aim is to follow what they have heard, cross beyond death.

26. What thing soever, moving or unmoving, is born, do thou know it to be from the union of the Field and Field-knower, O Bharata chief.

27. He sees who sees the Supreme Lord seated the same in all creatures, the Indestructible in the destructible.

28. Indeed, seeing the Lord seated the same in all he degrades not the self by the self, thence reaches the Highest Goal.

29. And he sees who sees actions are

wholly done by Nature, and the self is a non-actor.

30. When he sees the varied creature-natures rooted in the One, the expansion being only therefrom, then he realizes Brahma.

31. This Imperishable Supreme Self, being without beginning, being without attributes, neither acts nor is contaminated, O son of Kunti, though resting in the body.

32. As all-pervading ether being subtle is not contaminated, so everywhere seated in the body the self is not contaminated.

33. As the one sun illumines the whole world, so the Lord of the Field illumines the whole Field, O Bharata

34. Those who, with the eye of reason, see the difference between the Field and

Field-knower, and the (means of) liberation from creature-nature, they go to the Supreme.

Thus, in the Upanishad of the Glorious Divine Lay, the Science of Brahma, the Ordinance of Yoga, the Discourse between the Glorious Krishna and Arjuna, the Thirteenth Chapter entitled "The Yoga of Wisdom about Nature and Presiding Being."

CHAPTER XIV

The Attribute Triad

The Glorious Lord said: I will again declare to thee the Supreme, the highest of wisdom; knowing which, *munis* have gone hence to supreme perfection.

2. Relying upon this wisdom they, acquiring a conformity to My righteousness, have no (further) evolution at creation nor troubles at its dissolution.

3. My womb is the Vast Brahma. Therein I place the germ. Thence is the birth of all creatures, O Bharata.

4. In all the wombs, O son of Kunti, whatever shapes are produced, the Vast Brahma is (to be deemed) their womb, I their germ-supplying Father.

5. Goodness, Passion, Darkness: these three Nature-born attributes, O mighty-armed, encompass the imperishable embodied one in the body.

6. Among these, goodness, on account of its freedom from impurity, bright and healthful, binds by attachment to pleasure and by attachment to knowledge, O sinless one.

7. Know Passion to be essentially affective and spring from thirst and attachment. It binds the embodied by attachment to activity, O son of Kunti.

8. But know Darkness as ignorance-born and a confounder of all embodied ones. It fetters by error, sloth and sleepiness, O Bharata.

9. Goodness develops into pleasure, Passion into action, O Bharata; but Darkness, on the other hand, enveloping

reason, develops into error.

10. Goodness appears overcoming Passion and Darkness, O Bharata; similarly Passion, overcoming Goodness and Darkness; likewise Darkness, overcoming Goodness and Passion.

11. When in this body knowledge-light appears at all the gates, then, be it known, Goodness is increased.

12. Greed, flowing energy, undertaking of actions, rufflement, desire,—these are born in increased Passion, O mighty Bharata.

13. Gloominess, idleness, error, also confoundedness,—these are born in increased Darkness, O son of the Kurus.

14. When during increased Goodness the body-holder goes into dissolution, he proceeds to the spotless worlds of the knowers of the Most High.

15. Going into dissolution in Passion he gets birth among the action-loving. Likewise vanishing in Darkness he takes birth in the wombs of the deluded.

16. The spotless fruit of well-done action is said to be *good*; but the fruit of Passion is pain and the fruit of Darkness, unwisdom.

17. Wisdom springs from Goodness, greed from Passion, and error, confusion and unwisdom from Darkness.

18. Upwards go the Goodness-seated, midway stop the Passionate, (while) seated in the movements of the lowest attribute downwards go the Dark.

19. When the discerner sees none other than the attributes as the actor, and knows what is beyond the attributes, he attains to My nature.

20. The embodied one, transcending

these three body-born attributes,
is released from the bonds of birth,
death, decrepitude and misery, and
tastes immortality.

21. Arjuna said: By what marks does
he appear, O Lord, above these three
attributes of what conduct is he? And
by what means does he transcend these
three attributes?

22. The Glorious Lord said: O
Pandava, light and flowing energy and
confoundedness, he who dislikes not
(these) when present nor seeks (them)
when absent;

23. Who, seated like one seated on
high, is not moved by the attributes;
who, knowing the attributes are moving,
stands still and stirs not;

24. Who is the same in pleasure and
in pain; self-centred; the same with a

lump of earth, stone or gold; the same with the agreeable and with the disagreeable; rational; the same amid censure and praise;

25. The same amid honour and dishonour; the same on the side of friend as on that of foe; he, a renouncer of all undertakings, is said to be above the attributes.

26. And he who serves Me with the help of unfaltering devotion, he, completely transcending the attributes, becomes fitted for Brahma-nature.

27. For I am the image of Brahma, the Immortal and Immutable, of Righteousness eternal, and of joy culminating in the One.

Thus, in the Upanishad of the Glorious Divine Lay, the Science of Brahma, the Ordinance of Yoga, the Discourse between the

Glorious Krishna and Arjuna, the Fourteenth Chapter entitled "The Yoga of Discrimination of the Three Attributes."

CHAPTER XV

The Highest Presiding Being

The Glorious Lord said: Unperishing is said to be the upper-rooted and lower-branched Ashwattha (fig tree) whose leaves are the verses (Vedas). He who knows this, is learned in the Vedas.

2. Downwards and upwards spread its branches, attribute-nourished and object-budding; while downward (from them) extend roots, following action into the world of men.

3. Nor is herein thus comprehended its form, nor its end nor origin nor support. One, cutting this firm-rooted Ashwattha with the hard weapon of non-attachment,

4. Should seek that Goal, reaching

which none return; and approach the feet of that very Primeval Presiding Being, from whom the ancient impulse has sprung.

5. Those that are free from pride and confoundedness, victorious over the evils of attachment, constant in Adhyatma, desire-pacified and liberated from the duals called pleasure and pain, go undeluded to That, the Goal Imperishable.

6. Neither sun, nor moon nor fire lights That, reaching which none return. That supreme position is Mine.

7. Of Myself, indeed, an everlasting portion, manifested as a creature-soul in the world of creature-souls, attracts the nature-seated senses, of which the mind is the sixth.

8. When the Lord goes into a body

and when he goes out, he takes these away as the wind, fragrances from (their) seats.

9. Seated upon the eye and the touch and the taste and the smell and also upon the mind, He enjoys objects.

10. Departing or even staying or enjoying attribute-endued, Him the bewildered see not, (only) the wisdom-eyed see.

11. Yogis by assiduity see Him staying in the self. Untrained thoughtless men, even with assiduity, see Him not.

12. The splendour of the sun, which lights the whole universe and that which is in the moon and that which is in the fire, do thou know that splendour to be from Me.

13. Pervading the earth I hold the creatures with My strength and

becoming the watery Soma I nourish all plants.

14. Becoming the fire sheltered in the bodies of the living, joined with the incoming and outgoing currents, I digest the four kinds of food.

15. And I am seated in every one's heart. From Me are memory, reason and belief. Indeed, I am the object to be known by all the Vedas, and I am also the Veda-versed expounder of the Vedas.

16. Presiding beings in this world are these two: the Perishable and the Imperishable. The Perishable includes all creatures; the unchanging is called the Imperishable.

17. But the Presiding Being Most High is another, called the Supreme Self who, as the Imperishable Lord,

pervading sustains the triple world.

18. As I am beyond the Perishable and even of the Imperishable, the Highest, so in the world and in the Vedas I am proclaimed as the Highest Presiding Being.

19. He who, unconfounded, thus knows Me as the Highest Presiding Being, he, the knower of All, is devoted to Me with all his nature, Bharata.

20. Thus the greatest secret, this Ordinance, is declared by Me, O sinless one. He who, understands this, becomes wise and duty-accomplished, O Bharata.

Thus, in the Upanishad of the Glorious Divine Lay, the Science of Brahma, the Ordinance of Yoga, the Discourse between the Glorious Krishna and Arjuna, the Fifteenth Chapter entitled "The Yoga of Highest Presiding Being."

CHAPTER XVI

Godly and Demoniac Endowments

The Glorious Lord said: Fearlessness, purity of heart, perseverance in knowledge and Yoga, almsgiving, sense-control, sacrifice, good reading, austerity, straightforwardness,

2. Harmlessness, veracity, wrathlessness, renunciation, peacefulness, freedom from calumny, compassion to creatures, non-greediness, mildness, modesty, unfickleness.

3. Energy, forgiveness, steadfastness, cleanliness, freedom from enmity and pride are his who is born unto godly endowments.

4. Vainglory, arrogance, conceit, wrath, also harshness and ignorance

are, O Partha, his who is born unto demoniac endowment.

5. The godly endowment is for liberation and the demoniac for bondage deemed. Grieve not, O Pandava, thou art born unto godly endowment.

6. In this world are two streams of creatures: the godly and the demoniac. The godly (stream) has been described at length. Hear from Me of the demoniac, O Partha.

7. The demoniac people know not when to follow an impulse or when to control it. Neither purity nor behaviour nor veracity is among them.

8. They say the world is without truth, without principle, without a governor, is evolved from the (union of) inferior and superior (principles), and what else

but the source of desire.

9. These of ruined selves and little understandings, adopting this view, become doers of fierce deeds as enemies for the destruction of the world.

10. Surrendered to insatiable desires, possessed with vainglory, conceit, and arrogance, and accepting impious doctrines from delusion, they engage in action with impious resolves.

11. Surrendered to innumerable schemes till death, deeming the gratification of desire as the highest aim, holding that to be all,

12. Tied to a hundred cords of expectation, having desire and anger for highest impulses, they unfairly seek accumulations of wealth for the gratification of their lusts.

13. "This I have gained to day; this

desire "I shall obtain; this wealth is mine; even this "again shall be mine;

14. "I have killed that enemy; I will kill "even others; I am the lord, I am the enjoyer; "I am successful, powerful, happy;

15. "I am possessed of wealth and possessed "of men; who else is my equal? I will perform "sacrifice; I will give alms; I will amuse,"—thus unwisdom-deluded,

16. Whirled by many thoughts, caught in the meshes of confoundedness, bent on the gratification of desire, (they) fall into an unclean hell.

17. Self-glorying, stubborn, intoxicated with wealth and honour, they irregularly perform nominal sacrifices with vainglory.

18. Sheltered in egoism, power,

haughtiness, lust and wrath, the malicious hurt Me in their own and others' bodies.

19. These cruel and wretched haters, the vilest of men, I continually cast into demoniac wombs in mortal worlds.

20. Fallen into demoniac wombs, deluded birth after birth, O son of Kunti, they, instead of attaining to Me, tread the lowest path.

21. Threefold is the gate of hell, destructive of the self: desire, wrath, and greed. Therefore, one should renounce this triad.

22. Man avoiding these three gates of Darkness, O son of Kunti, works out his own welfare, then reaches the Supreme Goal.

23. He who, rejecting the injunction of the Ordinance, follows the workings

of desire, he obtains neither success nor happiness nor the Supreme Goal.

24. The Ordinance, therefore, is the authority for what should or should not be done. Having learned what is declared in the rules of the Ordinance, thou shouldst act at this moment.

Thus, in the Upanishad of the Glorious Divine Lay, the Science of Brahma, the Ordinance of Yoga, the Discourse between the Glorious Krishna and Arjuna, the Sixteenth Chapter entitled "The Yoga of Godly and Demoniac Endowments."

CHAPTER XVII

The Triple Faith

Arjuna said: But, O Keshava, what is the position of those who, rejecting the injunctions of the Ordinance, perform sacrifice with faith? Is it Goodness? or Passion? or Darkness?

2. The Glorious Lord said: Threefold is the nature-born faith of the Embodied one: good, passionate and dark. Hear of it.

3. Every one's faith is in conformity with his nature, O Bharata. Man is constituted by faith. Of whatever faith he is, even that he is.

4. The good sacrifice to the gods, the passionate, to Yakshas and Rakshasas (spirits of wealth and greed); and the

others, the *dark* people, sacrifice to Pretas and Bhuta-groups (departed *and existing* creature-groups).

5. Those people who perform severe austerity, unenjoined by the Ordinance, with vainglory and egoism, and with desire-tinged vigour,

6. Foolishly torturing the element-group comprised in the body and also Me living in the inner body, do thou know them to be of demoniac resolves.

7. Food, dear to every one, is also threefold; likewise sacrifice, austerity, almsgiving. Hear this about their distinction.

8. Foods, conducive to longevity, goodness, strength, health, pleasure and satisfaction, succulent, oily, nutritive and cheering, are dear to the *good*.

9. Bitter, sour, saline, overhot,

pungent, dry and burning foods, productive of pain, regret and sickness, are liked by the *passionate*.

10. Food, which is stale, flavour-lost, putrid and spoiled, and even rejected and unserviceable, is agreeable to the *dark*.

11. The sacrifice, prescribed by rule, which is offered by non-seekers of fruit settling the will on sacrifice as a duty, is *good*.

12. But in consideration of fruit or also for the sake of even vainglory, when one performs sacrifice, O best of the Bharatas, do thou know that sacrifice to be *passionate*.

13. Without rule, without distribution of food, without a formula, without making a remuneration, without faith, the sacrifice is said to be *dark*.

14. Reverence to the gods, the twice-born, preceptors and the wise; cleanliness, simplicity, Brahma-conduct, and harmlessness are called bodily austerity.

15. Undisturbing speech that is truthful, agreeable and beneficial, and the practice of good reading, are called the austerity of the speech.

16. Cheerfulness of the mind, placidity, thoughtfulness, self-control, purity of sentiments: all this is called mental austerity.

17. This threefold austerity performed with superior faith by men undesirous of fruit and settled in Yoga, is called *good*.

18. That austerity, which is performed for the sake of obtaining good treatment, respect and worship, and also through

vain glory, is there called the *passionate,*—fickle and unsteady.

19. That austerity which is performed with mistaken avidity, with self-torture or for the sake of another's ruin, is called *dark.*

20. Gift that ought to be made, and is given to the unrequiting, having regard to the fitness of place, time and recipient, that gift is thought *good.*

21. But that gift is thought *passionate,* which is given for the sake of requital, or looking for fruit, or grudgingly.

22. That gift is said to be *dark,* that is given, at an unfit place or time, to undeserving objects, with unkindness and contempt.

23. "Om, Tat, Sat;" this is thought the triple index to Brahma. Therewith Brahmanas, Vedas and sacrifices were justified of old.

24. Therefore uttering "Om" are undertaken the Brahma-preacher's acts of sacrifice, gift and austerity, prescribed by rule.

25. (Uttering) "Tat" liberation-seekers without thinking of fruit perform acts of sacrifice and austerity and various acts of charity.

26. "Sat" is used for reality and goodness. The word "Sat" is also applied to commendable acts, O Partha.

27. Perseverance in sacrifice, in austerity and in almsgiving is also called "Sat." Action, for the sake thereof, is also called "Sat."

28. Without faith sacrificing, almsgiving, performing of austerity or whatever is done, is called "Asat" (not good). O Partha, it is neither for hereafter nor for here.

Thus, in the Upanishad of the Glorious Divine Lay, the Science of Brahma, the Ordinance of Yoga, the Discourse between the Glorious Krishna and Arjuna, the Seventeenth Chapter entitled "The Yoga of Division of the Triple Faith."

CHAPTER XVIII

Liberation

Arjuna said: O Mighty-armed, I desire to know the essence of Sannyasa (surrender), and, O Hrishikesha, O slayer of Keshi, also of Tyaga (renunciation).

2. The Glorious Lord said: Sages know as Sannyasa the surrender of (self-gratifying) covetous actions. The intelligent call the relinquishment of all action-fruit as *renunciation*.

3. "Action should be renounced as an evil," say some philosophers; others (say), "the action of sacrifice, almsgiving and austerity should not be renounced."

4. Hear, O best of the Bharatas, My decision about that *renunciation*.

Renunciation, O mighty man, is declared to be threefold.

5. The action of sacrifice, almsgiving and austerity should not be renounced: that, indeed, is a duty. Sacrifice, almsgiving and austerity are verily purifiers of the wise.

6. But even these actions should be performed after renouncing attachment and fruits. This My decision is the best, O Partha.

7. But the *surrender* of lawful action is not proper. The renunciation thereof from confoundedness is called *dark.*

8. When thinking it painful, one renounces action from fear of bodily suffering, he making a *passionate* renunciation obtains not the fruit of renunciation.

9. When renouncing attachment and

also fruit, one does nature-ordained action as a duty, O Arjuna, then the renunciation is thought *good*.

10. The renouncer, goodness-filled, intelligent and freed from doubt, dislikes not action when uncomfortable, nor likes it when comfortable.

11. Indeed, for one having a body it is not possible to renounce actions completely, but he that is a renouncer of action-fruit is called a *renouncer*.

12. The triple fruit of action,— desired, undesired and mixed,—is for the non-renouncer *hereafter*, but for the surrenderer *never*.

13. Learn from Me, O mighty-armed, the five causes producing result in all actions, mentioned in the Sankhya action-theory:

14. The body, the actor (will), the

various organs, the various distinct functions, and, among them as the fifth, the divine (cause).

15. Whatever the action, right or wrong, a man undertakes with body, speech or mind, these five are the causes thereof.

16. This being so, whoever by reason of unformed understanding sees himself as the sole actor, he the wrong-notioned sees not.

17. He whose nature is unegoistic, whose understanding is uncontaminated, he even slaying these people neither slays nor is fettered.

18. Knowledge, the object of knowledge, and the knower: threefold is the mover to activity. The appliance, the act and the actor: thus triple is the action-composite.

19. Knowledge as well as action or actor is from diversity of attributes declared to be threefold in the description of the attributes. Duly hear of them also.

20. Whereby in all creatures is seen one unperishing nature, the undivided in the several, do thou know that knowledge to be *good*.

21. But the knowledge that in all creatures perceives severally the manifold natures of different varieties, do thou know that knowledge to be *passionate*.

22. That, however, which is associated with a single effect as if it were the whole, and is unfounded, aimless and narrow, that is declared to be *dark*.

23. Regulated, devoid of attachment,

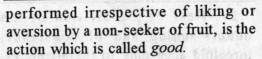

performed irrespective of liking or aversion by a non-seeker of fruit, is the action which is called *good*.

24. But the action that is done with much effort by a desire-seeker, or else by an egoist, is declared *passionate*.

25. The action one undertakes from delusion overlooking consequence, loss, injury and ability, is that called *dark*.

26. Liberated from attachment, unboastful, endued with constancy and zeal, unaffected by success or failure, is the actor called *good*.

27. Affected, solicitous of action fruit, greedy, harmful, impure, susceptible to exultation and grief, is the actor called *passionate*.

28. Inattentive, uncultured, stubborn, deceitful, misdoing, indolent, despondent and procrastinating is the actor called *dark*.

29. Hear of the division of the understanding and of constancy, threefold according to the attributes, (now) being declared without reserve with their distinguishing features, O Dhananjaya.

30. That understanding, O Partha, is *good* which knows what propension is good and what restraint is good, what can be done and what cannot be done, what is to be feared and what is not to be feared, what is bondage and what is liberation;

31. Whereby right and wrong, and also what can be done and what cannot be done, are incorrectly known, that understanding, O Partha, is *passionate*.

32. That clouded understanding, which thinks wrong to be right and all objects contrarywise, is, O Partha, *dark*.

33. Constancy that, unflinching by Yoga, compasses the functions of the will, vital currents and senses, that constancy, O Partha, is *good*.

34. But, O Arjuna, the fruit-seeking constancy that through attachment sustains virtue, desire and object, that constancy is, O Partha, *passionate*.

35. Whereby a dull-witted one shakes not off sleep, fear, grief, despondency and also recklessness, that constancy is thought *dark*.

36. Now then hear from Me of the threefold pleasure, O mighty Bharata.

37. That in which one, by practical training finds comfort and certainly reaches an end to pain, which is at first like poison and in the sequel like immortality, that pleasure arising out of the health of his understanding is called *good*.

38. That which springs from the contact of sense and object is at first like immortality and in the sequel like poison. That pleasure is thought *passionate.*

39. The pleasure that at first and in the sequel is self-confounding, that pleasure springing from sleep, sloth and error is called *dark.*

40. There is not the entity on earth nor again among the gods in heaven, that is free from these three nature-born attributes.

41. Of Brahmanas, Kshatriyas and Vaishyas and of Shudras, O dismayer of foes, the duties are divided by the attributes sprung from their respective natures.

42. Harmonizing of the internal faculties and of the external faculties,

austerity, purity, forgiveness, simplicity, knowledge, discrimination and belief are the nature-born functions of the Brahmana.

43. Heroism, energy, constancy, dexterity, and even daring in battle, almsgiving and domineering disposition are the nature-born functions of the Kshatriya.

44. Cultivation, cattle-breeding and trade are the nature-born functions of the Vaishya. The nature-born function of the Shudra is essentially subservient.

45. Each man engaged in his characteristic function gains perfect success. Hear, how one engaged in his characteristic function gains success.

46. Man wins success, because by performing his characteristic function, he worships Him from whom issues the

impulse of creatures and by whom all this is pervaded.

47. One's own characteristic duty, become worthless, is better than another's characteristic duty well performed. Doing nature-ordained duty one incurs no sin.

48. Connate function, O son of Kunti, should not be renounced even though faulty; for all undertakings are enveloped by evil as fire by smoke.

49. One whose understanding is everywhere unattached, who is self-subdued, who is without longings, he by surrender attains to the superior success of exemption from activity.

50. Learn from Me, briefly of course, O son of Kunti, how having attained to (this) success he reaches Brahma, which is the supreme position of wisdom.

51. Endued with refined understanding, regulating the self with constancy, overlooking the sound and other sense-objects, overcoming likings and dislikings,

52. Living is seclusion, eating abstemiously, regulated in speech, body and mind, always intent upon the Yoga of meditation, fully resting on dispassionateness,

53. Shaking off egoism, violence, arrogance, desire, anger and covetousness, considering nothing as his own, the tranquillized man is fitted for Brahma-nature.

54. Brahma-natured, cheerful-spirited, he neither grieves nor covets. Equable amid all creatures he acquires supreme devotion to Me.

55. By devotion he is instructed about Me, how and who I am in reality; then

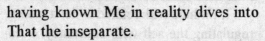

having known Me in reality dives into That the inseparate.

56. But if one is resigned to Me, he even though constantly performing all sorts of actions, attains through My grace to the Eternal seat undecaying.

57. With the mind surrendering all actions unto Me, esteeming Me supreme, taking the aid of the understanding, always fix thy mind on Me.

58. Having thy mind settled on Me thou wilt by My grace cross all difficult passes. But if from egoism thou dost not listen, thou wilt be ruined.

59. If sheltered in egoism thou thinkest "I will not fight," thy belief is, indeed, false. Nature will impel thee.

60. Tied to thine own nature-born function, O son of Kunti, thou shalt powerless do even that which from

stupefaction thou wishest not to do.

61. The Lord of all creatures dwells in the heart, O Arjuna, causing all creatures by His Divine Power to revolve as if by mechanism.

62. Unto Him go for shelter with all thy nature, O Bharata. By His grace thou shalt obtain supreme peace, the resting-place eternal.

63. Thus by Me is declared to thee wisdom, the secret of secrets. Considering this fully, do as thou likest.

64. Hear again the greatest of all secrets, My last word. Thou art extremely dear to Me, therefore I speak for thy good.

65. Fix thy mind on Me, devote thyself to Me, sacrifice unto Me, humble thyself before Me; thou shalt, indeed, come unto Me. Truly I avow to thee,

thou art near to Me.

66. Renouncing all duties come unto Me, the One Refuge. I will release thee from all sins. Grieve not.

67. This for thee. Not to the non-ascetic nor even to the impious nor to the unsubservient is this to be declared, nor to him that dislikes Me.

68. He that shall preach this supreme secret among My devotees, he (thereby) performing the highest devotion to Me shall come unto Me without doubt.

69. Nor shall there be among men any one doing a dearer service to Me than he, nor to Me dearer than he shall any other be on earth.

70. He who will study this our righteous discourse will be deemed to be worshipping Me with wisdom-sacrifice. Such is My decree.

71. The man who, with faith and without dislike, merely hears it, even he being freed shall obtain the good worlds of virtuous actors.

72. Hast thou, O Partha, listened to this with single-pointed attention? Is thy unwisdom-stupefaction destroyed, O Dhananjaya?

73. Arjuna said: My confoundedness is destroyed, and, O Unfallen One, I recollect myself through Thy grace. I am settled, free from doubts. I will do Thy bidding.

74. Sanjaya said: Thus, of Vasudeva and the great-souled Partha I heard this marvellous discourse causing the hair to stand on end.

75. Through Vyasa's grace I have heard this highest secret, the Yoga, from Krishna the Lord of Yoga, Himself teaching in my presence.

76. O King, remembering and remembering this holy marvellous discourse of Krishna and Arjuna I rejoice again and again.

77. And remembering and remembering that most marvellous Form of Hari, great is my wonder, O King, and I rejoice again and again.

78. Where Krishna is the Master of combinations, where Partha is the wielder of the bow, there, I am convinced, would be glory, victory, growth and firm morality.

Thus, in the Upanishad of the Glorious Divine Lay, the Science of Brahma, the Ordinance of Yoga, the Discourse between the Glorious Krishna and Arjuna, the Eighteenth Chapter entitled "The Yoga of Liberation."

NOTES
CHAPTER I

39. its ancient morality, the special rules of conduct or the characteristic morality in the form of rites and observances which distinguish one family or race from another.

40. the women being corrupt. The loss of moral tone in a decaying race is followed by the contracting of inferior connexions, the consequent confusion of progeny and the formation of inferior mixed races. The word "varnasankar" literally means *colour-mixing,* and a tainting or mixing of race-colour was viewed in Hindu society as a great evil, in as much as the distribution of duties among classes by which the social mechanism was carried on might be affected to the detriment of social arrangements. Hindu society recognized only four primitive classes distinguished by colour and characteristic qualities often found associated with it. The white Brahman, the red Kshatriya, the yellow Vaishya and the black Shudra possessed respective characteristics settling their respective positions and duties in society. Intermarriages, though allowed, were limited by legalizing such marriages as took place between men of a superior class and females of an inferior class and generally assigning to the off-spring the status of the mother's class. Offspring of superior mothers and inferior fathers, as well as offspring born out of wedlock, were held to be *varna sankar* who could not be incorporated in any of the recognized classes and naturally caused social anxiety for their provision. Even at the present day, purity of race-colour is sought to be maintained with equal care and watchfulness in many enlightened nations, and a white woman taking a black man for husband would incur greater odium than a white man taking a black wife. The reason probably is that a man has greater opportunities than a woman of improving and elevating children of mixed descent who would otherwise only swell the number of inferior population beyond manageable limits.

41. offerings of food and drink. The pious offering of food and drink to deceased ancestors is the expression of a sentiment which merely differs in form from what is to be found in other nations in the shape of a portrait or a statue or an architectural monument or an endowment. The periodical rites of the Hindu are at least calculated to keep alive the hereditary characteristics of his family, and it is held, not without plausibility, that the discontinuance of these pious observances are apt to diminish the virtues by which the ancestors were, as it were, maintained in their exalted position. The father lives in the son, and the son's deterioration is held to be the father's deterioration. The loss of characteristic hereditary virtue is no common loss, and anything calculated to maintain it cannot be an objectionable ceremony, which, besides, strengthens the filial sentiment and incidentally helps the poor through the distribution of food or other necessaries. At the basis of primitive institutions there is a good deal of imagination with which philosophy has never agreed even in India, but what real substance there is in anything need not be thrown away with the husk.

The Gita contains no express approval from Krishna of the institution of *Shraddhas,* or of the hypothesis on which Manu bases their obligatory character. On the other hand, the Pitris like the gods are lightly held wherever they have been alluded to.

CHAPTER II

7. instruct me. It was a settled rule with teachers to cast no pearls before swine, but to impart spiritual instruction only to the deserving and really earnest. The principle on which this rule was based recognized no real aptitude in a man whose heart was not pure enough to realize any notion of Divinity other than what was compatible with, or favourable to, his ideas of personal happiness. The Teacher in Gita expresses a different opinion by which the One God is held to be accessible to all. The necessity, which led the great sages to think a preliminary polytheistic training was desirable for the reception of the monotheistic doctrine, is not appreciable by us at this distance of time, and we see that at the date of the Gita the necessity had ceased and the gods had been brought under the dominion of Nature's laws (vide XVIII. 40).

11. neither for the dead nor for the living. The Sanskrit word, *gatasun* and *agatasun* mean *divested of bodily or organic vitality* and *not divested of organic vitality* respectively, and therefore exclude reference to the *spirit*

or *soul*. The soul being the real self of the man, philosophers do not grieve over the body whether living or dead.

12. never was a time when I was not. This hypothesis of God's eternal existence and similar existence of subordinate souls (often called creature-souls) rests on the infallibility of the Lord's word. Belief in the existence of both the inner self and its cause is, according to some, due to innate conviction, and the indestructibility of spirit being conceded, the proposition declared in the verse cannot be denied.

13. as the Embodied One. Passing *out of* the body is as *natural* as the passing from stage to stage *in* the body, and the reflective man feels his soul is unaffected by the change called *death* which, in fact, is a stage often interpreted to mean "So the acquisition of another body."

14. sense-contacts, *matra sparshah*
is the Sanskrit expression. Some
consider the second word *sparshah*
means the "objects of the senses," viz.,
sound, touch, colour, taste and smell.
Others think all these are varieties of
touch referable respectively to the
peculiarities of the different senses.
Every sense gives not only *a knowledge*
but also a *feeling of pleasure or pain*
which is in character transitory, and the
reflection that it is transitory can best
enable one to be patient and overlook
it, (vide Manu 11. 96), and acquire
habits of endurance and equanimity for
cool contemplation and realization of
one's immortal nature.

16. certainty of the Unreal. The
words *sat, asat, bhava* and *abhava* are
important. The sense of the passage is
that the *asat* or "unreal" can not be

unchangeable or permanent, and one cannot be certain for two moments about pleasure or pain or even the concrete body itself, while the *sat,* the real, the spirit in the body, cannot perish,—one cannot imagine that it perishes: at least, one who understands matter and spirit, assigns mortality and immortality as their distingushing characteristics. Hence one's *real* concern is his soul and considerations of *bodily* pain or pleasure should not influence his conduct where his soul's welfare may be jeopardized.

17. know That to be indestructible & c. The words *"That"* and *"this,"* for *tat* and *idam* in the original respectively refer to the *creature-soul* and the *body,* or, according to some, to *God* and the *Universe.*

18. the bodies of the Embodied one. The plural *dehah* as referred to one body-holder is accounted for by holding

(*a*) that the Universal Soul is in reality the *apparently many* creature-souls in different bodies; or

(*b*) that the Universal Soul being ubiquitous is present in every body as President over the creature-soul (XIII. 22); or

(*c*) that *dehah* means the component *limbs and organs* of a body; or

(*d*) that a living person has three bodies, viz.

1*st*. the inner *causal body of primitive ignorance* which separates *spirit* from *matter;*

2*nd*. the *subtle or linga* body composed of *mind and five senses* (XV.

7-10), or according to some, of understanding, mind, five senses, five active organs (hands, feet, speech, and the two excretory) and five vital forces (prana &c.); and

3rd. the gross or outer tangible body of flesh and blood.

This verse unmistakeably refers to the *creature-soul,* but the word "creature" does not imply *creation out of nothing,* which is the Christian idea of *creation.*

22. goes into other new ones. The doctrine of transmigration of the soul from body to body is approved by the Gita because it strengthens the sense of personal responsibility for one's own acts. Vide, however, v. 28.

23. neither weapons cleave &c., verses 23, 24 contrast the nature of the soul with that of the body. "all-pervading" means *pervading the entire body*.

27. for sure is the death of what is born, nothing material is unchangeable, but even then, nothing is annihilated by death; so that, if the soul is only subtle matter and dies with the body, it is not annihilated and simply assumes a new form which when manifested is its re-birth. Physical things are constantly decomposing and recomposing by the inherent force of Nature.

28. Creatures. *Bhutani* means "those which come into being" or "manifestation" and includes the *elements, bodies* and *all perceivable objects* and occasionally, *sentient or conscious beings in their perishable aspect.*

29. This, the *soul* or true inner self as distinguished from *creatures* referred to

in v. 28; and it is declared to be a *marvel*
because nothing in the external world
is like it, and neither philosophy nor
shrutis can make it intelligible. One can
only *feel* it in himself.

31. own duty. The word *Swardharma*
means "the duty peculiar to a person or
class of persons" on account of special
aptitude due to birth and training in a
particular family or class. The physical
and moral qualities, for example,
inherited by a Kshatriya boy and
developed by special training, indicate
his natural fitness for the warrior's
occupation, and a choice of another
vocation would have been, in old Hindu
Society, treated as a shirking of duty. The
principle on which the Hindu castes
came to be established may no longer be
applicable under altered circumstances
when by an all-round education and free

intercourse between nations, the characteristic differences between individuals and races are on many points vanishing, but classification in some form or other is unavoidable, and the doctrine of *swadharma* will still be applicable in that form.

38. **Equally prepared for pleasure &c.,**—this refers to the mentally balancing one's self on Right, which precludes sin.

39. **the Sankhya,** that which pertains to the rational wisdom about body and soul. Kapila, the first philosopher (*adividwan*) or expounder of the philosophy of the Vedas, held that the Universe is the manifestation of an active principle called Nature, in relation with an infinite number of souls, whose superiority or inferiority depends upon

the extents of their respective powers to control or to resist the influences of the various forces of Nature. The gods of the Vedas and men were held to be intrinsically similar, in being subject to the laws of Nature. The Sankhya philosophy is either the atheistic philosophy of Kapila, or the theistic one, *the Yoga philosophy* of Patanjali.

The Yoga. *Yoga* ordinarily means *union* but often signifies, as here, *Karma-Yoga,* that is, *the union through activity to the Supreme.* When activity is disciplined in view of *personal* enjoyment, it is *passionate* or self-regarding *Karma-Yoga.* When the discipline is due to a sense of obedience to Natural or Divine *laws, i.e.* to a sense of duty or Right, then it is *dispassionate* or moral *Yoga* which the Gita commends.

41. the right deliberate understanding, viz. that understanding which apprehends *rightly* by virtue of education and skill acquired through practice in frequent acts of reasoning and deliberation. Man's faculties often err. The eye, for example mistakes in a desert a mirage for a plantation, and a closer inspection dispels the *error.* At another spot, the eye seeing an oasis may err the other way or may *doubt* its own veracity. But frequent experience may educate the eye to detect the *fine* differences between a mirage and an oasis, and thus avoid both *error* and *doubt.* Thus every faculty of knowledge may be educated to supply *accurate* knowledge, and the same rule holds with the understanding also. The word *Vyavasay atmika* means "duly educated" or "correctly discerning" and an understanding, thus educated, forms a *single* belief which prompts the will to *right* activity.

44. for these &c., desires and passions and cravings for enjoyment make the moral sense *shaky*. The word *samadhi,* according to some, means "the soul" or "Great Soul"; according to others, "meditation" or "contemplation" or "fixity of principle."

45. for their object the attribute triad. Nature is held to consist of three attributes or propensities called *sattwa, rajas* and *tamas* which rule the gross and subtle bodies of man as well as external nature, though they predominate one at a time, keeping the remaining two in check. Selfish desire is roused by objects for the gratification of these attributes, and hence the "attribute triad" really represents *selfish* *desire*. The means of overcoming this *attribute triad* or *desire* are declared in this verse to be the formation of certain habits of body and mind, viz.

1st. to be *nirdwandwa,* i.e. to be *free from* the influence of the *duals,* called pleasure and pain, heat and cold, &c., in other words, to be able to endure than (for the sake of duty).

2nd. to be *nitya sattwastha* or always settled in the attribute of *satwa* or *right perception and goodness,* thus holding the other two attributes in subordination.

3rd. to be *nir Yogakshema* or careless about one's own wants and support, *i.e.* of acquisition and protection in a self-regarding spirit. The object then should be to direct activity in other-regarding spirit except what is necessary for maintaining the power of activity for the above purpose.

4th. to be *atmavan* or *full of the Great Self* or resting on Him fully, in a spirit of resignation, in thought, word and deed; or, according to some, to be *firm in conviction* or *unerring* or *unconfounded*.

This verse is an epitome of the teachings about human conduct to be found later on in the book.

46. Whatever the use of all-flooding water for drinking &c. The verse has been variously interpreted, the word *udapana* meaning both "water-drinking" and a "tank;" and "sarvatah samplutodake" meaning (1) "an extensive lake," or (2) "over-flowing with water on all sides" or (3) "everywhere being covered with water."

Some of the accepted interpretations secured by adopting different grammatical arrangements of the components of the verse are,

(*a*). A wise Brahma-devotee resorts to all the Vedas for minor purposes of life just as, while possessing a vast lake, he would for minor purposes use a tank.

(*b*). A wise Brahma-devotee finds in all Vedas a scope for his natural activity for various useful purposes, just as when in possession of an over-flowing tank, finds ways of distributing his surplus water into useful channels.

(*c*). A wise Brahma-devotee, for the employment of his natural

activity, chooses suitable
portions of he Vedas, just as
when in bodily thirst he would
only use a small quantity of
water from a large lake, and
that from the point where the
water is pure.

(*d*). A wise Brahma-devotee makes
no use of the Vedas just as he
would not use a tank
submerged in high floods.

Reading this verse with verses 45 and
47, one gathers the sense to be that the
Vedas are good in so far as they
prescribe lawful acts, but are illusory or
at least unacceptable, in so far as they
hold out prospects of tempting rewards
and foster the growth of the self-
regarding or selfish desires.

48. Settled in Yoga, the essence of

Yoga is the *mental equipoise* and *not the outer result* of success &c.

49. Far inferior to this Yoga of the understanding &c. The word "action" is held to mean here "action with a personal motive of gratification and enjoyment." This special meaning of "action" is needlessly adopted. The *Yoga of the understanding* is the *mental equipoise* or *sense of Right* referred to in v. 48, and this verse compares the values of the *outer act* or *result* and the *inner sense of Right*, and declares the inferiority of the former.

50. whether well-performed or ill-performed, one moved by a *sense of Right* transcends the consequences of *clever* or *clumsy* performance.

51. Renouncing the action-born fruit, a conscientious actor, free from a personal motive and irrespective of considerations of his low or high birth, rank &c., finds an inner satisfaction or stage of peace.

52. When thy understanding &c., when reason can overcome the temptations of the desires and passions, then is a true apprehension of precepts possible. The word *Nirvedam* is often held to mean "indifference" or "sense of inutility" (of the precepts).

53. well-informed by hearing. The word *shruti-vipratipanna* is explained by some as "bewildered hitherto by hearing or various shrutis." The word *samadhi* here may mean either *fixity or stability of the Yoga or moral understanding,* or *the self or Great Self.*

55. stable understanding, here defined to be that condition in which the conscience is unshaken by objects of desire, however tempting, and gives the man an inner satisfaction in his obedience to it, and a complete disregard of external objects of gratification as a motive.

56. Muni, literally a thinker or meditator, but usually used for a *thinker equable in the midst of disturbing circumstances* referred to in the verse.

57. understanding settled, the avoiding of voluntary selfish attachment, and the absence of elation or depression from external accidents constitute this understanding.

58. When from sense-objects &c., i.e. when he has the power to control the natural *affective* impulse of the senses.

59. Sense-objects etc. The word *rasah* literally means *taste* and secondarily, *liking for external enjoyment.* The sense-objects are *sound, touch, colour or form, taste and smell.*

61. should sit aiming at Me. The power of keeping sense-solicitations in check depends upon the strength of the conscience or Yoga-understanding, and this again depends upon love of God, or of the model character of the age, as the best embodiment of the best idea of God then possible. This is the *supreme* referred to in v. 59.

64. There being cheerfulness etc. Cheerfulness or mental health or harmonious activity implies freedom from disturbing influences, and therefore a scope for the understanding for cool reflection and comprehensive belief.

66. One unsettled in Yoga etc., without equableness the right understanding and reflection are impossible, and without reflection peace or permanent happiness is impossible.

68. whose senses are withdrawn etc., the phrase "all round" is used to signify only this much that *the senses no longer make their various solicitations* but *not* that *their sense-perceptions become closed.*

69. the restrainer, the word *sanyami* means the *enlightened muni* of the 2nd line. *Sanyama* is an *application of the mind* through a sense to a *particular* object or point by efforts of attention called *dharana, dhyana* and *samadhi,* meaning respectively the "mental grasp," "close examination or contemplation" and "the mental absorption and self-forgetfulness in the true significance of the object." When all these three phases of attention are applied to the same object, the mental condition is *enlightened understanding*. Hence a *sanyami* or restrainer is the *muni* of enlightened wisdom, who has controlled the natural fickleness and roving, pleasure-seeking disposition of the mind, and is *blind* or insensible to the attractions of worldly pleasures, which the man of the world sees. The *muni,* by education and correction of nature, acquires the *light of wisdom,* while the undisciplined man moves in the *light of desire*.

70. **He gains peace,** the natural causes of pleasure and pain are ever present, but they do not affect the *muni's* tranquillity.

72. **repose in Brahma,** the condition in which the flame of worldly desire is

quenched by the all-absorbing idea of Brahma. To suppose this implies *absorption in the substance of Brahma* which is spirit, would be to make an interpretation not warranted by the word *nirvana.* All that the qualifications of moderation, unselfishness and humility, referred to in v. 71, seem to lead to, is a *conformity* with Brahma which holds the Universe on its path of harmonious progress.

CHAPTER III

3. a two-fold path. Man's welfare, humanly speaking, depends upon *his voluntary activity* and his *knowledge,* but different estimates of their *comparative* efficacy have often been made. A class of philosophers advocate the *Yoga of Action;* and another, the *Yoga of knowledge.* The former are *Yogis,* or

Karma-Yogis, and the latter, *Sankhyas* or *Sannyasis.*

·6. **controlling the organs of action etc.,** activity being indispensable for acquisition of knowledge and skill (v. 4), or at least for the support of life (v. 50, suppression of physical activity while the mind is active is but a self-deception and hypocrisy.

8. **nature-ordained action,** that action which nature or Divine law ordains as *lawful.* Niyata literally means "regulated" and includes *nitya* and *naimittika* (explained in not to XVIII. 2).

9. **action for the sake of sacrifice,** *sacrifice* is not an exact equivalent of the Sanskrit Yajna used in the text. Yajna means *worship,* but the emblematic form used from ancient times in India is associated with *Fire,*

the first named of Vedic gods, which being fed by adequate fuel is held to maintain the vitality of the universe with various energies distributed along innumerable channels. In the *Samhitas* and *Brahmanas,* Fire was held to be the pervader of the Universe and the distributor of nourishment among gods and men or other creatures, and latterly Vishnu was *Yajna* or Lord of *Yajna.* The grand circulation of energy going on in the Universe is due to the action of fire fed by adequate fuel, and *Yajna* seeks to be an imitation of the action of Nature by feeding the flame or flames, i.e. natural appetites and desires in creatures, as for example, the sense-flame with the fuel of sensible objects (sound, touch, taste, form and smell), the feeling-flame with pleasure and pain, the understanding-flame with knowledge, and so on. A man feeding these flames in himself and others obeys God's laws as manifested in the laws of external nature, and this obedience is only complete when his devoutness expresses itself in the predominance of the altruistic over the egoistic sentiment. Hence, besides sacrifices prescribed for special occasions or seasons, five great sacrifices are enjoined upon a Hindu for daily observance, and thus all his activity is to be devoted to worship throughout life in the form of sacrifice. The five great sacrifices are—

(1) **Brahma-Yajna** or the giving and taking of spiritual knowledge stored in the Vedas or books of sages.

(2) **Deva-Yajna** or distribution of food and necessaries of life in honour of the gods.

(3) Pitri-Yajna or similar distribution in honour of departed ancestors.

(4) Nri-Yajna or hospitality to a man in need of it.

(5) Bhuta-Yajna or feeding of domestic animals &c.

Thus the religious sentiment is the basis of Hindu morality, however unrefined the detailed workings of that sentiment may be. Morality of the highest order may be found in men *without* any religious sentiment, but Hindu morality cannot be independent of it.

10. The Lord or offspring, etc. Verses 10-12 cite Vedic authority to support the doctrine of sacrifice. The Vedic gods are lightly held in the Gita, and subordinated to natural attributes or impulses. The gods were spoken of as presidents over the various organs of man and the respectively corresponding objects in external nature; and as the Gita assigns these functions to the forces or attributes of Nature, the injunction of *Prajapati* about sacrificing to the gods is approvingly quoted simply to show that the Vedic form contains the spirit of the doctrine of sacrifice which is meant to foster the habit of mutual help and support in society. To sacrifice to the gods is to help others, in whose organs the gods preside.

13. eating at the completion of sacrifice, a house-holder after completing the five great sacrifices (note to v. 9) may eat for his own sustenance and renewal of his strength to enable him to continue his other-regarding duties day by day. The *spirit* of the rule, apart from considerations of the *necessity* or *feasibility* of *literal* compliance at the present time, is to be noted.

14. From food come creatures into being etc., verses 14 and 15 declare that it is God's energy which circulates through the Universe, and that sacrifice is his method or medium for the distribution of such energy. Unless, therefore, man adopts this method, society will be at a stand-still (v. 9) from mere self-regarding activity.

15. Brahma sprung from the Imperishable. The **Brahma** means (1) the Vedas, (2) *Brahma*, (3) *Nature*, (4) creature-soul. The 3rd meaning is best applicable here.

The **akshara,** and in the 2nd line, **all-pervading Brahma** are used for the First cause. The word **Brahma** literally means *the Vast*.

17. who is really devoted to the self, verses 17 and 18 point out the impossibility of self-centring without dependence on any external object and therefore of acquiring a complete respite from activity. This sense of the passage is clear from the tenour of v. 19, which emphasizes the excellence of right activity as a means of attaining to supreme perfection.

20. By action, indeed, Janaka and others, etc. Societies are held together by acts of mutal help, and a disposition to activity is indispensable for the maintenance of society and should have the support of illustrious actors for the guidance of the masses. The *passive* doctrine of some *shrutis* and floating philosophical opinions are here discountenanced.

24. the author of deterioration, etc. The word **sankara** means a *mixture* or *taint* by which a race or society may be *degraded* by neglect of the natural law of activity.

25. so unattached the wise should act, etc., he should uphold the cause of activity for the sake of the masses, by the performance of righteous actions, which not only *directly* benefit others but also furnish examples for imitation.

26. One should not unsettle etc., the ignorant work from personal motives, still they *work.* The real distinction of the wise consists in the unselfishness and righteousness of their motives, and *not* in the *kind* of work which is very much the same in both cases. The wise should not discourage actions but perform lawful actions to induce the

NOTES 203

masses to imitate, and, by habitual
performance of lawful acts, to gradually
acquire and develop their sense of duty
or Yoga-understanding.

27. Acts are fully done, etc., the
outward act is due to the powers of the
physical organs stimulated by the
external world into activity. The egoist
attributes all this to himself or to his
stimulated volition, which again is not
the whole cause. If the volition be held
no part of the true self, the act is possible
only by the physical organs having the
requisite power and the external world
supplying the stimulus; and thus the true
self is not *directly* connected with
the act.

29. Those that are deluded, etc.,
until one feels the superiority of the
spiritual over the physical nature, he is

hardly fitted for the Yoga-understanding or the doctrine of conscience in its full strength; and unless he has learned to control his desires and passions, he has no idea that the true interests of his real self are little benefited by external enjoyments. Conscience is best fostered by directing *activity to good works*. Idle precepts do not avail much.

30. Surrendering all actions unto Me, etc. Both the impulse, and the corresponding external object are God-ordained, and therefore activity is natural and approved by God. Circumstances of daily or occasional occurrence which stimulate activity are likewise attributable to the same cause, so that the performance of duty under the circumstances is only doing the behests of god. When a Cincinnatus or a Wellington or a Nelson, though averse to bloodshed, goes out to fight, he does so under a sense of duty or a divine command inferred from the necessity of the occasion. Ver. 32 condemns all philosophy which ignores active morality. *Vide* also verses 19 and 31.

34. One should not come under their power, etc., the measure of the strength of the moral sense is the measure of one's power to resist the solicitations of the senses which interfere with duty.

35. One's own characteristic duty, etc. The right choice of a vocation in life is discussed in Bhagavat Purana, Book X. Chapt. 24, verses 13-18, and a well-defined *Swadharma* may not be impossible under the altered circumstances of present time (vide note 11. 30). A Nelson or a Wellington might be aptly addressed in this way if sought to be a clerk or a priest.

37. It is desire, etc., the desires of the flesh, which being thwarted are converted into *wrath,* are the real cause of sin.

42. That, the pronoun sah is put for the *Soul* or *true self.* According to some, it stands for *desire, the enemy* (Hebrew *Satan*), seated in the senses &c. (v. 40)

43. controlling the self by the self. Atma (Self) means (1) the individual body or, as now called, the pictorial self;

(2) the Ego of sense;
(3) the Ego of volition and attention;
(4) the Ego of understanding or reason;
(5) the creature-Soul;
(6) the Universal Soul.

At one end of the chain is the external

world and at the other the Universal Soul, and the verse enjoins No. 5 to be loyal to No. 6 and hold Nos. 1 to 4 subservient, and thus avoid all desire for external enjoyment. A sense of Right, subordinated to religious piety, can control this hierarchy of Self and exterminate the influence of desire.

CHAPTER IV

3. My devotee and comrade. A *shruti* (Mundaka III. 3-5 Shwetashwatara III, 6 and 7) describes the Supreme Soul and the creature-soul as two comrades like two birds on a tree (likened to the body).

6. Though unborn, etc. The divine incomprehensible power, called *Maya,* is here declared to enable the Supreme Lord with all the attributes of His nature, to appear in a human form which, like every other creature-substance, is liable to birth and death. The Incarnation of God is an unintelligible mystery and must rest upon faith, for scientific reason cannot be assigned for it.

7. Whenever there is deterioration of virtue, etc. The verse defines the proper time of an incarnation, viz. when the *positive* force of virtue is so overcome by the *negative* one of vice that it cannot set itself up.

9. He who really understands My birth, etc., one who believes the Incarnation was meant to raise fallen virtue and give it a new vigour, adopts that model with a view to regeneration and growth and exemption from re-birth, *i.e.* fresh trials and experience of *mortal* life, or rather, similar to those of mortal life.

10. Divested of desire, fear, etc. A devout adoption of the model purges one of his desires and passions, and lifts him up to the perfection of Godly nature.

11. Howsoever men, etc. Activity, knowledge or feeling, whichever may be a man's characteristic tendency, if subordinated to piety or if earnestly conforming to the model, will meet with a response from the Lord. Some interpret the verse to mean that He favours a devotee exactly in correspondence with his motive, (*i.e* selfish or unselfish), though a selfish devotee is usually in error in sacrificing to *other gods* (v. 12), attributing quick worldly success to *other gods* and *not* to the inherent nature of activity in the production of fruit.

13. The fourfold race-colour, etc. The formation of what are called *castes* was evidently due to a distinction of race-colour (no inconsiderable mark of distinction even in modern times): and characteristic qualities, usually found in the various races of different colours, defined and settled the characteristic functions of each in society. In one sense God is the author of this distinction among the classes in that society but the *direct* cause is man's own nature, of whose movements God is a dispassionate spectator (non-actor). Vide v. 14.

18. He who sees inaction in action, etc., action is a good *lawful action* (positive), **misaction** is a *bad harmful act*, and **inaction** is *abstention from action* when the action is of the latter class **(misaction)**. The performance of *action* as opposed to *misaction,* so that *action* and *inaction* (*i.e.* good action and non-performance of bad inaction) respectively amount to *persisting in good* and *avoiding evil,* which are said to help each other reciprocally and constitute the *Yoga-understanding.* One so disposed is an intelligent Yogi who performs every action subject to the dictates of that respectively imply the *active Nature* or the Universe and the inactive or *conscious Spirit,* and the sense of the passage then is that the man who sees God in the Universe and the Universe in God is the most intelligent Yogi and worker.

19. **He whose undertakings, etc.,** the consumption of action in wisdom-fire refers to wisdom-sacrifice (v. 27), and a *pandita* is a man of such (true) wisdom.

23. Action performed for the sake of sacrifice, etc., such action fetters not the actor because it is a disposition of *natural activity* in obedience to the law or command of God.

24. Brahma is the act of offering. Sacrifice, as already explained, is a disposition of the active energies in obedience to divine law; and therefore one, who sees the manifestation of divine energy in all the constituents of a sacrifice (viz. instrument, act, the offerings, fire and the sacrificer), really finds his resting-place in the Great Spirit.

25. sacrifice to the gods. The Vedic gods are but personified natural forces or divine laws regulating the functions of the organic and inorganic world. Distribution of food and material wealth

for relieving the needy was the main
characteristic of this sacrifice, at the
same time contributing to social
gatherings and fostering good feeling
and community of thought and action.

**Some pour (this) sacrifice into
Brahma-fire, etc.** This is explained
variously as follows:—

(a) To offer sacrifice (creature-soul)
  to Brahma;

(b) To sacrifice by sacrificing to God
  (*not* the many gods);

(c) to offer the prayer-sacrifice
  ("Om") by speech-sacrifice to
  God i.e. to offer prayer in words
  taking the name of God (Om
  being the original or first name
  of Brahma).

However interpreted, this line refers
to sacrifice to the one God by offering

up one's whole soul or by humble prayer or taking His name.

26. Some pour the senses, etc., some control the sense-impulses when duty requires to acquire the habit against future occasions.

Some pour sense-objects, etc., some feed *others'* sense-fires with corresponding objects (sound &c.) for their training or healthy enjoyment.

27. Some pour all sense-functions, etc., some regulate functions (of senses, active organs, vegetative organs of life) by means of *enlightened, harmonious* application. *Yoga* being a mental equipoise and rectitude, the regulation referred to is one which merges in or subserves an enlightened sense of duty.

28. Some ascetics, etc., those who perform the various sacrifices described in verses 25-27.

29. Some whose highest aim, etc., an even movement of the lungs co-exists with a state of deep attention, and it is held that by producing a condition of even movement of the lungs, one can fix attention and reflect and meditate with advantage. The *inward* and *outward* currents of breathing are alternate, the *inward* coming to a *pause* when it changes into the *upward* direction, and similarly the *upward* coming to a *pause* before changing into the *inward* direction. These two *pauses* or stops are called *Kumbhakas, inner and outer.* It is supposed that increase in the duration of the *Kumbhaka* (especially the *inner*) is effective in the augmentation of the power of mental concentration and dispassionateness. The popular impression on this point is not tested, and, as there is nothing in the Gita to justify it, all that seems to be meant is that the inward and outward efforts should be equalized. (Vide also v. 26).

Some regulated in food, etc. The vital powers or *pranas* are—

(*a*). **Prana** or the power of taking in food including inspiration of air;

(*b*). **Apana** or the power of discharging excreta including expired air;

(*c*). **Udana** or the power of throwing up of solids, fluid or gas in vomiting, belching &c.;

(*d*). **Samana** or the power of distributing nourishment in the body;

(*e*). **Vyana** or the power of muscular contractions and expansions in various limbs, as in movements of lips, eyelids, &c.

These five *pranas* or vital forces are
sustained by food, in which are
supposed to reside recouping vital
forces. The practice of orthodox Hindus
before commencing their meals is to
take in five nominal morsels, while
uttering the words *pranaya swaha,
apanaya swaaha, etc.* The vital forces
have the common fire of *hunger* into
which the vitalizing food is offered, and
this sacrifice is meant for the support
and health of the body and to enforce
regularity and guard against excess. A
fanciful, but generally accepted,
interpretation of this passage is that the
five senses are gradually consumed or
merged one after another in their next
higher ones by gradual withdrawal of
nourishment. Some would apply this
verse to the *Khechari mudra i.e.*
introducing the tongue into the gullet

after cutting the fraenulum with a very stupid result.

30. These sacrifice-knowers, etc., the habitual self-control and regard for others' wants, which worship in the form of sacrifice induces, lead up to divine perfection. **Amrita** in the 2nd line means the *residue of food after distribution at a sacrifice,* and this residue is *material* in the case of material sacrifices and *sentimental* in the case of spiritual sacrifices at which spiritual food is distributed or imparted.

32. spread out at the mouth of Brahma, *i.e.* prescribed or declared in the Vedas (Brahma), or held as indispensable for introduction to the Brahmic idea, or performed in the presence of Brahma (God).

3. perfect action, Karmakhilam in

the original may mean *the group of actions comprised in a complete sacrifice,* or may mean the *complete sacrifice* which concludes in wisdom (v. 35).

35. see all creatures,...in the self, then in Me, *i.e.,* realize the entire creature-nature (mortal and immortal) in thine own self and its dependence on Me.

38. The Yoga-perfected one, etc., the righteous activity, called *Yoga,* of itself produces in the mind the *wisdom* which sees the affinity of creatures through a Common Parent or the Primitive Cause.

40. Ignorant and wanting in faith, the doubter, etc., if doubts continue from ignorance or distrustfulness of this wisdom (vers. 35, 38), they deprive one of all happiness. Even in every day life activity is possible upon some beliefs being held about material phenomena, though such beliefs are often liable to be displaced by further experience or new discoveries of science. In the matter of moral piety, error is avoided by reason of the correctness of the data, viz., the absolute certainty about one's selfhood, its direct dependence on the Great Selfhood or Primitive Cause, and personal feelings directly known. Second-hand knowledge and common sense cannot, however, be altogether done away with.

41. Whose actions are surrendered to Yoga, etc., the activity subordinated to the Yoga-understanding or sense of Right and to faith resulting from the wisdom which realizes the brotherhood of man and the Fatherhood of God, cannot fetter the actor because his motive is pure and unconnected with his own self.

CHAPTER V

2. the Yoga of action is preferable, etc., surrender of action in an unenlightened spirit of resignation is a futile attempt at the beginning. Hence *lawful* activity is preferable.

4. The (common) fruit of both, peace or joy which is the *common* fruit of both.

6. But Yogaless Sannyasa, etc., lawful activity ensures experience, dispassionateness, moral strength and *practical* skill. But mere *unpractical* contemplation or reasoning, without the requisite *practical* knowledge or development and stability of character, would be a waste of mental labour. It is the *moral thinker* who realizes Brahma.

7. He who is Yoga-endued, etc., the root of evil is desire or covetousness, and *not* activity. Activity cannot harm the self-controlled and large-hearted man. **sarva-bhutatma-bhutatma** means *one* who realizes others' feelings as well as they themselves do. (*vide* VI. 29-32).

10. reposing actions in Brahma, etc., in doing acts *appropriate* to an occasion he simply does God's behests like a servant, furnished by Him with the necessary instruments in the shape of natural impulses and powers to meet the occasion. Whatever the *apparent* character of the act may be, he commits no sin thereby, because he considers it to be *right* and in obedience to God's command.

11. the simple senses. The sensitive and active faculties are both included in the word *indriya,* and the adjective *kevala* means *single* or freed from affection or aversion. A Yogi's action is meant to purge the self of all selfish desires and passions by *right* practical application of all his faculties in the affairs of life.

13. like a victor, the Embodied One, etc., one who has conquered his desires and passions is a victor. When he has *refined* his faculties by Yoga and they have become *competent* and *loyal* servants, he then, as it were, mentally assigns the charge of all actions to them without any further troubling himself about the *doing or directing* an act. The faculties would then be doing the right thing spontaneously.

14. The Lord. The word *Prabhu* in the original means the *Lord of the body* or the *Lord of the Universe*. In the former sense, he is distinct from the material bodily nature which, with its impulses and activities, produces the fruit of action. In the latter sense, the word *swabhava* has to be interpreted as Universal Nature.

15. The Manifold Being. *Vibhu* like *Prabhu* of the preceding verse is applied both to the *creature-soul* and the *Great Soul*. The literal meaning is "variously manifesting," which the *creature-soul* is through every faculty and the *Great Soul* through all his works in the Universe. The soul is essentially pure and spotless, but from some unknown cause it becomes associated with a body at birth. At that time it is only conscious of the external or changeable world and *not* of its unperishable nature. This external knowledge is styled *unwisdom* or *ignorance*, the knowledge of the true nature of the self being then wanting.

16. But those in whom, etc., *Vide* IV. 35.

18. Pandita, a man of true wisdom, who feels for the meanest of creatures as well as for the highest, and finds evidences of God's power and care *equally* in both.

19. Even here is birth conquerer, etc., An equal eye for all is a divine characteristic. A man who has an equal eye for all transcends the artificial barriers of birth, station and accomplishments.

27. equalizing etc. *Vide* note IV. 29.

The following recipe for worry cure published in a western magazine may be profitably compared with V. 27—29 and VI. 10—15:—

"When the symptoms of worry begin to manifest themselves, when your mind gets to dwelling upon some one troubling matter with feverish insistence, when you find yourself depressed or irritable or overstrung or full of foreboding, then go into your room and lock the door.

For the first application of this prescription you must be absolutely alone and in silence; after a while you may be able to make these conditions for yourself anywhere by the complete withdrawal of your mind even in the midst of a crowd, but at first you must be quite alone. Loosen your garments completely and lie down in the most restful position you can assume. The one I recommend is flat on the back, with the shoulders as low as possible, and with just enough elevation of the head to be comfortable.

Avoid raising the head too high, thus cramping the neck and impeding the circulation. Now close your eyes for a few minutes and, raising the arms, let them fall and lie loosely and naturally above your head. Lie thus for a minute or two, then begin to take deep, long breaths, as deeply as possible, exhaling quietly and naturally. Keep this up for five minutes, until you are sensible of a real relaxation and refreshment of the body. You will then be in the physical condition to take up the mental work.

Begin this process by making the mind as empty as possible for the moment. Figure to yourself that your mind is a slate over which you pass a damp sponge, obliterating every line that the day's thought has made upon it. Wash the slate as clean and blank as you can, and then begin to impress upon its face a new series of thought. First say to yourself, not loud but quietly and with your whole mind fixed upon its meaning, "This is God's world, not mine." Say it over and over, not in a wandering, parrot-like way but understandingly, until the full meaning of the phrase has flooded your mind and brought with it a delightful sense of calm and rest.

With the above may also be compared the prescribed processes of physical and mental washings at the daily *sandhya* of a Brahmana at morning and evening. The differences on points of detail are due to differences of social conditions and habits."

28. **Ever free, indeed, is he, etc.** The

freedom referred to is the freedom from desires, passions etc., fitting the Yogi for the spiritual conception and feeling of God's power, intimacy and love (v. 29).

CHAPTER VI

3. For a muni climbing up Yoga, etc. For the education, refinement, dispassionateness of the physical and mental faculties, it is necessary to perform *lawful acts*. This would be necessary for a *rising muni*. When he wants to be a *Yoga-established* muni, he must pacify and regulate the inner springs of activity and hold them in check except for a lawful purpose. Habit of *right activity* must be supplemented by the habit of *right thinking* and *feeling*. An enlightened Yogi has no personal motive to gratify. *Vide* v. 4.

6. to one, conquered by the non-self, etc. anatma is *not-self* of external objects. Inclination for external sense-gratification is a disaffection to the self and is hostile to the real interests of a man.

14. Being self-serene, etc., the condition to be secured for concentrating attention and meditation, are not to be so continuous or engrossing as to exclude social intercourse or physical activity in every day life. *Vide* verses 16, 17 which provide for all due requirements of a healthy life. A mathematician, astronomer or chemist even has to secure some of these conditions for making correct observations, so that additional care in regard to moral observations is expedient.

15. This constantly fixing the self, etc., the wise Yogi attains to peace and resignation in God, which become part and parcel of his mental nature, even in the midst of active engagements which are unavoidable in life. By **nirvana** is meant the *extinguishment of the worldly thirst* for gratification and lordship.

25. should not think of anything (else), *i.e.,* he should keep all distracting thoughts out of his mind. To suppress thought-power or make a vacuum of the mind is neither possible nor here enjoined. A common misinterpretation of Patanjali's first aphorism is the root of the prevalent misconception about Yoga. Ver. 26 clearly indicates what *thinking of nothing* means, and vers. 29-32, which describe the highest perfections of the Yogi, lose all meaning if will or thought-power is to be destroyed.

29-32. One whose self is settled in

Yoga, etc., the Yogi in contact with
Brahma (v. 28)—

    (*a*) sees every creature resting in
          God (v. 29);

    (*b*) realizes the relationship between
          the creature-soul and God, and
          never forgets the intimate
          relationship on account of piety
          from one side and grace from the
          other (v. 30);

    (*c*) serves God as an Omnipresent Unity
          by serving his creatures (v. 31);

    (*d*) views others' pleasures or pains
          as if they were his own (v. 32).

That the doctrine of Yoga is not
directed towards the suppression of the
thought-principle is clear from the
above, which define the highest
condition of the Yogi.

    41. finds birth in the house, etc. The

doctrine of transmigration is not now in favour, but no doctrine, which pretends to deal with matters lying outside of the bounds of human knowledge, has any surer basis than human imagination or revelation.

The claim of a doctrine to acceptance depends upon the extent or degree of its consistency with reason, and it is alleged that, judged by this standard, the doctrine of transmigration is no worse than many a religious dogma accepted by some of the most enlightened nations of the earth. The personal responsibility of every one for his actions is the basis of the doctrine of transmigration. It holds that the present diversities in life are due to acts in a prior life, for nothing else can be imagined, without imputing partiality to the Almighty, to account for such conditions as congenital blindness mutism or lunacy, birth in an immoral family, race or society, absence of opportunity for spiritual or other instructions, conditions fostering positive immorality from infancy, unmerited pain from congenital leprosy or other troublesome disease, or again natural intelligence, or piety or similar advantageous conditions, etc. The doctrine of transmigration, however, in the absence of proof, must rest on *faith*. Whether it has done anything to strengthen the sense of individual responsibility or further the cause of social virtue, it is not easy to decide in the present condition of society.

46. The Yogi is greater than the ascetics, etc., freedom from selfish desires and passions constitutes the Yogi's superiority over other classes of seekers for improvement.

47. Of all Yogi's again etc., the pious Yogi who does God's works (vers. 31, 32) is, however, the highest of Yogis. Piety and dutifulness are the highest characteristics of a Yogi, and *not* quietism and mental vacancy as are generally supposed.

CHAPTER VII

1. **to the utmost,** as far as possible; or in My outward Universe-emanating aspect.

6. **I am (cause of) the manifestation, etc.** After referring to the Lord's two energies or powers emanating respectively *matter or force* and *spirit,* which constitute what is called the *material cause* of the Universe (vers. 5, 6), this verse speaks of Him as the

instrumental cause. In other words, a third energy is declared as combining and dissolving the two components of the *material* cause. In some theologies these three energies are merged into one, the Divine Will, which is assumed to have created the Universe out of nothing. But though expressed in an apparently different form, the hypothesis implies that the Divine Will has the latent germ or *something* in a potential form which develops into this tangible Universe. About the *nature* of the Final cause, rational philosophy has nothing to say. Human curiosity, not unoften morbid, provokes study of the nature of final causes but comes back disappointed. The Universe with its innumerable contents of forces and forms is conceived as a *unit*, and as causation is a necessary idea of the mind it naturally seeks to trace the Universe to *one Final cause*. The mind ultimately arrives at such a cause by successive generalizations, of which the highest ones contain factors more or less hypothetical. Those factors, concreted by imagination, differ in different countries on account of the diversities in natural scenery and forms and habits of thought. The extent of difference about these higher factors of generalization is often so great that it is hopeless to bring about a consensus of opinions on purely rational grounds. In a matter like this (the *nature* of the Final cause), the best guide is a man's own inner light, and mere doctrines can be of little avail.

7. On Me is woven, etc. This verse is often misunderstood. The *apparent pantheism* should be corrected by reference to the expression in v. 12, "but not that I am in them or they are in Me," and also to IX. 4, 5.

8. I am flavour in waters, etc. The various instances of the manifestations of the Primitive cause do not inculcate a pantheistic idea. To speak of the cause in terms of the effect is not unusual. When, for example, we say of a copy of the Paradise Lost or Comus that this book is Milton, or of a copy of Geometry that it is Euclid, we do not mean that these books are Milton or Euclid bodily; but we mean that they are the productions of Milton or Euclid, and that they best manifest what Milton or Euclid was, though the mind and body of Milton or Euclid are no longer in the land of the living.

12. those that are good-natured, etc., these creatures, though created by

God, are distinct from Him. This declaration, however, does not remove the difficulty felt by those who hold that there is nothing in the effect which was not in the cause in a potential form; and the rationalistic doctrines cannot perhaps be free from some tinge of pantheism.

13. the world seeks not to know Me, etc., the desires of the flesh are too strong for the generality to dispose them for any thought about the ultimate source of all objects of desire.

14. this attributeful power, etc., the power is divine, which has created the charming relations between bodily susceptibilities and the external world. And it is here declared that man of his own unaided effort, without seeking divine help in a spirit of true resignation, can never overcome this power.

Atheistic moralists of course do not accept this dictum, and Sankhya reformers and their Buddhist followers are the most prominent of them.

17. The wise man, etc. Wisdom is here shown to consist in dispassionate activity and devotion to the One (God).

29. Brahma, also called *Tat* (That), is literally *the vast, the all-comprehensive. Param* meaning *supreme* is often prefixed to denote the Highest Brahma as distinguished from *Brahma* or *Mahad Brahma* which means the *Primitive Nature of Force* which manifests the Universe in its present real from.

Adhyatma, the presiding self of the Universe, or the Omniscient who, as Paramount Self in the body, sustains the creature-soul.

Akhila karma, the grand *yajna*

(sacrifice) of God through the activity of Nature or *Mahat* which evolves and dissolves the Universe (vide III. 14 and 15); also interpreted by some as *all action or duty.*

40. Adhibhuta, perishable or changeable characteristic of Nature (material). According to some, the Lord of beings or inanimate creatures.

adhidaiva, the bright, perceptual or conscious nature. According to some, Lord of the gods, *i.e.* Brahma.

Adhiyajna, the President over the sacrifice or *yajna* which carries on the work of Nature, in the Universe as a whole or in each individual body.

CHAPTER VIII

3. Own (inner) nature. The Sanskrit *Swabhava* means *own* or essential nature of Brahma which is the Paramount Personality or Selfhood.

creature-natures or *bhuta-nature i.e.* something brought out into manifestation.

4. Here in this body, etc. The purport of vers. 3, 4 is this: The First Cause viewed as an Eternal, all-pervading Essence, is called *Param Brahma,* and viewed as the Paramount Spirit or Selfhood, is called *Adhyatma.* From Adhyatma emanates energy or creative activity called (*akhila*) *karma,* causing the birth of *bhuta* or creature nature, of which the perishable constituent is called *adhibhuta* and the conscious constituent is called *purusha.* The Personal God Himself is called *Adhiyajna* who sustains the relations between the *adhibhuta and purusha* and their joint and several relations with the external world.

5. remembering Me in his last moments, etc. It is held (v. 6) that the mind improves or degenerates by reason of the saturation day by day with the paramount idea which rules a man's life. The mind thus undergoes a metamorphosis and is characterised by that idea even at the time of the man's death. The mind does not die with the disintegration of the body and accompanies the soul in its afterstate, as to the nature of which doctrines differ. According to the law of mental metamorphosis, the mind which holds the idea of *Adhiyajna nature* as its ruling idea, entitles the possessor to a nature similar to that of the *Adhi-yajna,* the characteristic of which nature is to *relieve, sustain and guide creatures.*

7. remember Me and fight. The

occasion was one when the *duty* of Arjuna was to *fight*, but that duty should be founded on a disposition of both understanding and will in conformity with the model nature, the *best* of the time in *moral* and *intellectual* worth. The precept inculcated in *shrutis* (vide Taittiriya. Bk. 1. chap. II. 3, 4) is that the highest in wisdom and behaviours should be the model of behaviour for his time; and as no better can then be possible, the soundness of the rule is evident. The incarnation theory stands upon the same basis, with this difference that the influence of the incarnate affects substantial *changes* for the better, and is far-reaching in extent and duration.

15. **having attained to Me, etc.,** the highest (model) man of his time is the worthiest for imitation, and one attaining to his nature attains to the

highest then possible. *Rebirth* in the verse means *falling back into mortal or sinful nature*.

22. devotion that is undeviating, does not adequately convey the meaning of *ananya* (literally *not-other*) which is *very intimate, own.* The devotee's relation to God should be closest intimacy. He should be the *dearest and nearest* to heart.

25. lunar light, light which is dim and variable with the waxing and waning of the moon. It is the type of the condition of the selfish or self-regarding *Karma-Yogi* who succeeds in attaining enjoyments and pleasures which are felt in a state of consciousness, from which the daylight of reason is absent.

27. becoming cognizant of these

paths, etc., the path of wisdom and the path of self-grafication lead respectively to the *infinite* and the *finite*. A Yogi whether self-regarding or not, has to forego immediate enjoyments and to exercise self-control, so that in the matter of discipline there is no appreciable difference. That being so, when a Yogi knows of both paths he has no hesitation in choosing the path of wisdom. The *Shrutis* describe in metaphorical language the different stages on these paths and the provision of imaginary guides to help the traveller on. *Spiritual* journey, described in this manner, need not be understood *literally*.

28. **passes beyond all that, etc.** A reading gives *abhyeti* and the meaning then is "attains all that."

CHAPTER IX

5. Nor again, etc. This verse clearly distinguishes *divine* from *creature-nature* and discourages the pantheistic idea.

13. Godly nature. *Vide* XVI. 1-3.

16. I the Vedic sacrifice, etc. Verse. 16-19 should be read with v.5, and must be held to describe the Divinity with reference to prominent objects, acts and sentiments in a variety of causal aspects,. Just as an author is described in terms of his productions which show his talents.

21. the Triple, trayi means *the Vedas,* probably because *Rik, Yajus* and *Saman* were the substantive ones, and *Atharvangirasa* was a later supplement. The Vedas were latterly held to be *inferior* learning (*vide*

Mundak 1.Chap. 1.v.5), inferior as being *nor* spiritual or monotheistic.

22. For them...I carry the burden, etc., the mere natural wants of a devotee, indeed of every man, are few. The devotee does not trouble himself about them, and they seem to be provided for by direct divine agency,.

23. other gods, the Vedic gods, before they were shorn of all their powers by the Sankhya philosphers, were apparently held to constitute a celestial Board with Vishnu or *Yajneshwar* as their President. **Other gods** are therefore the inferior gods driving authority and support from the President, and a sacrifice to be regular was to be made to the President and *not* to the powerless Board which must submit the matter to the President for disposal.

28. Sannyasa and Yoga, Yoga is *positive* work, and Sannyasa is *renunciation* or *abstention* in the shape of self-control, or *work* in a spirit of resignation to God.

29. Alike am I, etc., alike means *evenly just,* as the next line clearly shows.

30. impermanent, etc. This is a toilsome inconstant world. Everything is transitory in it and there is much misery besides, unless by doing God's works peace is obtained through His grace. *Vide* vers. 31, 32.

CHAPTER X

5. characteristics. The word *bhavah* is here used for *positive* or *elevating* characteristics or dispositions, as apposed to *abhavah,* negative or lowering dispositions.

11. seated in their characteristic, quickening and enlightening the characteristics and dispelling error.

41. fragments of My Splendour, these are brilliant manifestations of divine energy, and do clearly exclude the Pantheistic idea.

42. Pervading this whole, etc., declares the *intimate* and *watchful* care of God, and discountenances the idea of His *equality* or *identity* with the Universe by the use of the expression "part of Myself."

CHAPTER XI

46. four-sustaining, the word **chaturbhuja** means *four-armed, four-sustaining* or four-enjoying. The story in the Bhagavat Purana of Krishna being born as Vishnu's incarnation with four arms, two of which he withdrew at his father's request, accounts for the general adoption of the meaning *four-armed*. But the expression "that other form" in v. 45 implies Krishna's *two-armed* form, the expression "sceptred, and discus-in-hand" in v. 46 refers to *two instruments* for *two hands,* and the expression "Thy gentle human form" in v. 51 clearly shows that Arjuna wanted to see, *not* the four-armed but the *two-armed* form. Hence *four-armed* is an incompatible meaning. Virtue, gain, gratification and liberation are said to be the *four fruits* of the *Kalpa-tree* (representing the life of the Universe), and it is held that a being in human form is best equipped for preserving and enjoying these fruits. The adjective **chaturbhuja** is consistently interpreted as expressing the excellence of the human form for its aptitude for the four classes of fruits referred to.

55. He who, etc., by reverent imitation he acquires the active and passive virtues of the Man-god.

CHAPTER XII.

1. Which are the better instructed in Yoga, the subject of enquiry is the comparative efficacy of worshipping the Man-god and worshipping the invisible Brahma. *Upasana* is the directing and fixing of attention in a reverential attitude of the mind.

2. adore Me with the highest faith, the devout imitator or the Man-god is the higher Yogi, for the Brahma-worshipper attains to no higher perfection, even with all his self-control and public benefactions. The utility of the best and most comprehensive example is much greater than abstract precepts in morality and religion.

5. Greater is the trouble, etc. The divine representative in man's heart is his conscience which is an effective guide in many matters, but is not unoften baffled in circumstances of exceptional temptation or complexity. The unknown God is declared to be an *entity without any attributes,* and can thus never possibly shed any light on the path of his devotee who, unless specially gifted, is liable to frequent mistakes with his unaided conscience and some abstract religious dogmas.

6. But those who...adore (Me), etc., devout attention leads to a conformity with the model by a due adjustment and exercise of all internal and external faculties. Ver. 7 describes the resulting condition of stable peace, from which there in no falling off.

8-11. Fix thy will, etc. The methods by which to secure conformity with the highest or model character are—

(1) to dispose the understanding and will to accord with the model;

(2) in default, to learn to make the disposition by repeated efforts or practice;

(3) in default, to perform acts approved by Him and thus involuntarily obtain the desired success in respect to the inner springs and motives;

(4) in default, to be self-controlled and to dismiss all motives of reward for actions in the hope of attaining to His nature, (or in full trust in Him as to the efficacy of self-control and unselfish

action enjoined by this verse 11.)

12. Perception is certainly better than (blind) practice, etc., the sense is that a blind repetition of efforts is not so important as the true or intellectual grasp of the significance of the act through the different stages of reflexion and judgement. The desire of action-fruit, *i.e.* personal motive of reward will then be eliminated and peace will at once follow.

20. But exceedingly dear to Me, etc. The highest elevation of character consists in a loyal adherence to all the rules of conduct and disposition referred to in vers. 13-19.

CHAPTER XIII

2. know Me as, etc. The Paramount Self is Omniscient, and is thus the Chief

President in each body, the creature-soul being the Vice-President. The mind (including understanding, egoism, memory and will, etc.) is held to be material though subtle and more permanent than the gross or outer body and to be a sort of a medium of communication between the creature-soul and the external world.

5. Vast creatures, creatures used in the sense of *things created.* The *vast creatures* are primary imperceptible elements of matter (ether, air, heat, water and earth,) which being mixed up in different proportions form the *gross elements* perceptible to our senses.

the unmanifested, the primitive energy or power called Nature or Inferior nature of the Paramount Self. (VII. 4, 5.)

11. **wisdom,** Spiritual wisdom including rational knowledge, moral rectitude and piety.

12. **the Beginningless Brahma.** The original may be interpreted as *the beginningless Brahma culminating in Me,* but then *Brahma* must mean *Nature* to which the epithet *attributeless* (v. 14) is inapplicable.

20. **Regarding effect, etc.** *Nature* or *Energy* is the cause of activity, while the conscious soul is the cause of susceptibility to pleasure and pain. The mind is the subtle or fine organ through which the soul has this feeling and the physical faculties are moved to action.

21. **The Presiding Being, seated in Nature, etc.** The soul and body are so intimately connected that the affections and impulses of the body are felt by the soul as its own.

22. The Spectator and Appraiser, etc., but in this body there is another superior President who sees, approves, tests and sustains righteousness, and He is the Supreme Soul or God Omnipresent and Omniscient.

23. He who thus knows, etc., a clear discriminate wisdom about the two Presidents and Nature with her attributes ensures a condition, from which there is no fall (re-birth).

26. What thing soever, etc. The hypothesis, that all organic life comprises spirit and matter in different proportions, is not without plausibility. The absence of conscious life in the vegetable kingdom is held to be apparent only; for, when life does not subsist in animal organisms after the conscious element has escaped, it is argued that, vegetables live or die according as their conscious element is present or absent. Some plants even simulate the operations of a conscious being, and in regard to some it is in dispute as to whether they should be classed with the vegetable or with the animal. But after all, the declaration in the verse is a hypothesis, the truth or falsity of which does not affect the main doctrine of One Cause for all the various manifestations in the Universe, whether they be spiritual or material, or partly material and partly spiritual.

30. the varied creature-natures rooted in the One. The word Brahma is apparently used for the twofold Nature (VII. 5) of God, which really means the *energy* or *power* of God as distinguished from His transcendentality.

32. As all-pervading ether, etc, the wise man's self, though, like every other man's self, pervading the whole body, is yet untouched by its functions A man with strong desires and passions is apt to forget the essential distinction between body and soul, but the wise man always remembers it through all stages of happiness or misery.

33. As the one sun, etc. This simile is meant to illustrate how the Glorious Supreme Self lights and stimulates activity in each and every field.

34. the difference between the Field and Field-knower, *i.e.* between material Nature and the soul of two kinds, the Supreme Soul and the creature-soul.

Chapter XIV

2. conformity to My righteousness. The limit of reach is explained in the

2nd line, *viz.* immunity from the failings of *mortal* nature, *i.e.* what birth and death entail. By *attaining divine nature* (*or perfection*) is *not* meant that, powers of God which create and uphold the Universe are attainable.

3. the Vast Brahma. The Sanskrit Mahad Brahma as distinguished from *Param Brahma* implies infinite extension in space and time, in and through which any form of thought becomes possible. It is only in intense feeling that the ideas of space and time are lost; and that is the *rationale* of the proposition declared in the 2nd line of XIII. 20.

5. Goodness, Passion, etc. (*Vide* note 11. 45). The Sanskrit words Sattwa, Rajas and Tamas have not exact quivalents in English. Sattwa is the cause of knowledge or goodness or pleasure, *viz.,* that which is *intellectually true, ethically good, just or right,* or *substantially pure or transparent.* Rajas is said to be *ragatmaka,* and *raga* means *colour* as well as *passion* or *affection.* Rajas, differing from the pure *sattwa* in possessing a superadded *tinge* or *affectiveness,* is held to be the cause of *activity.* Tamas, literally *darkness,* is a negative attribute, meaning an *incapacity* for the other two and asserting itself in *sleep, indolence, mental confusion* and *error.* These three attributes are held to pervade all material nature including the faculties acting and the external world acted upon.

19. attributes as the actor, etc., all activity is due to the impulses of the body in correspondence with the external world. When on appropriate occasions a man can be outside the influences of the bodily attributes which act in concert with external nature, without identifying himself with them, he rises up to divine nature, subject to the limitation of v. 2.

25. a renouncer of all undertakings, etc., one who undertakes nothing on his *own* account for personal enjoyment or even support. (*Vide* IX. 22).

26. Serves Me, disposes activity in obedience to the Divine Will, by harmonizing himself with the fundamental laws of Nature.

27. I am the image of Brahma, etc. The Lord declares himself to be the representative of the Supreme Brahma in respect of certain characteristics, *viz.,* immortality, virtue and joy. The qualifying epithets seem to indicate that a part of Brahma-nature is not the proper object of imitation. The Bible, with reference to vindictive acts, makes a similar exception. "Vengeance is mine" is a saying attributed to God.

CHAPTER XV

1. the verses (Vedas). The Vedas or verses (*chhandas*) figuratively represent the leaves of the the great *ashwattha* tree (here the Universe). *Shwa* and *ashwa* respectively mean *spirit* and *matter* or *material nature*. The sacrifice called *ashwamedha*, described as *Kraturat* (highest sacrifice), takes its name probably from this meaning of *ashwa*, or at least, was latterly understood to typify a sacrifice of the entire material or animal nature of man. *Ashwa* may also mean *transitory* or *perishable, not lasting till the morrow.* The *ashwattha* tree is thus the *material* or *perishable* aspect of the Universe which, in spite of constant changes in it, is, however, unperishing as a whole. This tree is described as covered and protected by the Vedas fostering human desires for enjoyment. The tree is also described as *upper rooted, i.e.* issuing from the divine energy (Nature) or God, and he is declared to be a Veda-knower who knows the origin and support of the allegorical *ashwattha.*

2. its branches, etc. The various creatures, animate and inanimate, ranged in classes and subclasses, form the branches of the allegorical tree; and lower down, roots are described as stretching along the paths of activity in the human world.

7. Of Myself, an ever lasting portion, etc. *Vide* VII. 4, 5. The union of the *Superior* with the *Inferior* nature is here described. The five senses and the mind constitute what is called the subtle or *linga* body which, according to some schools of philosophy, comprise 17 constituents, *viz.* understanding, will, 5 sensory faculties, 5 active faculties, 5 organic forces (*pranas*). A spark of the Superior Energy of God sent by His Will to mingle with His Inferior Energy, becomes the creature-soul possessed of a mind and senses for a *permanent* body, besides the gross body which perishes at natural death. For all practical purposes, the mind is part of the true soul, and is called material because of its fickleness and changeability, which are incompatible with the recognized idea of the true inner self or soul.

8. takes these away, etc., the mind and senses, as already said, form a sort of a permanent sheath for the soul until its liberation or the imaginary collapse of the Universe during Brahma's night.

16. Presiding beings in this world are these two, the body (gross and subtle) is a president in the world, ruling and enjoying it, but it is *perishable*. The true self or creature-soul is the *unperishing* president in the body. Some hold that the *perishable* and *unperishable* presidents are meant to apply respectively to fickle *worldly men and unshaky men of faith and piety.*

17. But the Presiding Being Most High, etc. This verse leaves no room for pantheism, the express use of the word *anya* (another) unmistakably distinguishes the Supreme Soul from the creature-soul. The Supreme Soul is further declared to be the Lord who supports the triple world (*upper, middle* and *lower,*—applicable equally to the *macrocosm* and *microcosm*).

19. is devoted to Me with all his nature, etc. As an example or a model, the life of the Man-god furnishes the very best for imitation in the midst of the varying conditions of society, time and place one has to meet in the world. Devotion to Him, therefore, implies a zealous and persistent endeavour to imitate his perfections by *rightly* adjusting all *natural* conditions, physical and moral. (*Vide* VI. 31, 32, 47; IX. 34; X 9, 10; XI. 54, 55; XII. 8; XVIII. 65, 66)

CHAPTER XVI

8. They say, etc. This alludes to anti-vedic doctrines which hold that the

Universe is ascribable to no cause, that the assumption of the existence of One Eternal Almighty God is a mere verbal device to cover ignorance, and that the doctrine of divine government being the foundation of human morality has no other basis than pure imagination and selfish motive.

evolved from the (union of) inferior, etc. aparaspara-sambhutam may be interpreted in many ways, thus :—

(*a*) Not produced by reciprocities (of spirit and matter).

(*b*) Produced by the union of the *inferior* (matter) and *superior* (spirit).

(*c*) Evolved by the *inferior* (matter) into the *superior* (spirit).

However interpreted, the expression ignores divine agency.

18. hurt Me, disregard the Supreme Self, Spectator, Guide, etc., in the body (as described in XIII. 22).

21. desire, wrath and greed, *thirst for enjoyment* or means of enjoyment, is desire; *obstructed thirst* becoming violent is wrath; *thirst* on the point of gratifying itself is greed.

23. Ordinance. *Shastra* is *that which disciplines, i.e.* regulation or code or rules of human conduct resting on authority, human or divine.

CHAPTER XVII

3. Man is constituted by faith. The real or essential personality of a man is dependent upon the character of his faith; so that he is *good* if his faith is *good*, he is *passionate* if his faith is *passionate*, he is *dark* if his faith is *dark*.

6. and also Me, etc., weakening the conscience, etc., (XIII. 22) in which form the Supreme Soul is a guide and supporter in the body.

28. Without faith, etc., prescribed 'acts' done *with faith*, whether mistaken, desire-tinged or enlightened, cannot be infructuous, and must at least produce personal satisfaction; but if done *without* faith, the acts become *asat*, become *nought* here or hereafter.

CHAPTER XVIII

2. Sannyasa, Tyaga (renunciation). Actions are classified as—

(1) *Nitya* including *naimittika*, which are *lawful* or ordained by Nature or God.

(2) *Kamya* or self-gratifying or self-regarding, *ie.* with personal motives of worldly wealth, honour, growth of

family, etc. (The *pratishiddha* or prohibited class of actions, such as cruelty, murder and the like, is an inferior appurtenance to the *Kamya* class.) The essence of *Sannyasa* is the renunciation of *acts of the 2nd class*. If the *personal motive* be wanting, the same acts may be *nitya* or lawful, and *Tyaga* seeks to renounce the *self-regarding motive* irrespective of the *superficial aspect* of the acts by which their classification is regulated. Therefore the *Sannyasi* avoids acts classed as *Kamya* from their outward aspect or ostensible characteristics, while the *Tyagi* avoids acts which, however, classed, are wanting in *inner worth* on account of the motive or intent. The *Sannyasis'* rule of conduct differs from the *Tyagis* rule of conduct in this respect, though the object of both being the same, both may be called *Sannyasis*.

7. surrender of lawful action is due to error of judgement which really thwarts the object of *Sannyasa*. (*Vide* note, v. 2.)

11. to renounce actions completely. Duty is imperative and no man, whether he be a *sannyasi* or *he be a tyagi,* can override the fundamental law of Nature on the plea of obedience to seemingly contrary injuctions of the Ordinance.

16. himself as the sole actor. The expression in the original is variously rendered, *viz.* (1) *the pure or true self as the actor,* (2) *the self as the sole actor,* (3) *himself (the man referred to in v. 15) as the sole actor,* (4) *the self, essentially unconnected or unconcerned, as the actor.* Meanings (1) and (4) assume that the creature-soul neither affects nor is affected by the material organism which acts; but the feelings of pleasure and pain and the consequent approbation and disapprobation of the creature-soul, cannot be denied to have indirect influence in modifying the character of activity.

17. whose nature is unegoistic, etc., moral guilt does not attach to a man who is unselfish and does not covet the wealth or honour of the world, even though he annihilate a whole army. Chengis Khan and Tamerlane are called scourges of the human race; but Wellington, Nelson, Washington, etc., though responsible for much bloodshed and slaughter, are called noble actors.

18. mover to activity. A perception is followed by a desire which prompts an act. Thus the *perception* of the *perceived* object by the *perceiver* is the motive to action.

20. one unperishing nature, etc., the final constant law or nature, arrived at by successive generalizations from a perception of the *agreement* of things, is attained by *good* knowledge.

21. manifold natures, etc., when *disagreements, peculiarities* and *exceptions* are noticed in classifications and generalizations, then the knowledge is *passionate.*

22. associated with a single effect, etc., limited uncomparative knowledge without any idea of cause or consequence.

23. Regulated, etc., *i.e.* action which is *duty*, which it is right to perform without reference to personal liking, disliking or reward.

30. That understanding is good, etc., it is *good* understanding when it approves the *doing* of *duty* and the *non-doing* of *wrong* and sees *fear* in the *bondage* of desires and passions, and *absence of fear* in *freedom* from the same.

31. right and wrong, etc., when, on account of personal motive or bias, one fails to see that *right* is *what should be done and wrong is what should not be done,* then the understanding is *passionate.*

35. constancy, unflinching by Yoga, etc., when feeling, bodily cravings and sense-solicitations are controlled for a *right* purpose, then the perseverance is *good.*

37. That in which one, by practical training, etc., initial training is often galling and like poison destroys immediate enjoyments and pleasures, but the happiness gained at the end is lasting.

38. in the sequel like poison, sensual gratifications are ultimately followed by pain and, often, by an incapacity for healthy enjoyments, physical or mental.

42. nature-born functions of the Brahmana. Self-adjustment with God and his creatures in thought, word and action, is the *Brahmana's* characteristic effort. Mere heredity without this *natural characteristic,* does not constitute a *Brahmana.* Similar is also the case of a *Kshatriya* without *natural bravery* and *generosity,* a *Vaishya* without *natural skill* in the creation and distribution of *wealth,* and a *Shudra* without *natural aptitude for subordinate service.*

Like the inelasticity of old organs of the body gradually approaching dissolution, the inelasticity of the existing caste-system is a premonitory sign of approaching collapse, which will be quite in accord with the expected working of natural laws, to some extent foreseen by Hindu sages of old.

45. engaged in his characteristic function, etc., *natural* peculiarities may be advantageously improved and regulated, but cannot be discarded. *Full* measure of success is possible only when characteristic traits are properly educated and developed for the benefit of society.

46. Man wins success, etc., a man's *natural* characteristic is, as it were, ordained by God for duties conformable to it. When he therefore employs his faculities accordingly, he conforms to the design of Providence, and this obedience is in fact worshipping God.

49. by surrender, etc. (For Sannyasa, *vide* v. 2. note.) The sense of the passage is that class or characteristic functions are in themselves neither superior nor inferior, provided they fit a man and he performs them from a sense of duty, which gradually eliminates the selfish or self-regarding instinct, and ultimately precludes all improper impulses to activity from arising. This condition of the mind enables the *sannyasi* to be completely resigned to God in respect of his personal comfort or happiness (here or hereafter), though in regard to lawful duties he is not neglectful.

50. (this) success, the condition of one who has, as it were, finished his allotted task (ordinarily when unfitted for further active duty, by reason of age or infirmities,) is one of absolution from duty, just like what is earned in the public service of a State by a superannuated functionary.

51-53. Endued with refined understanding, etc. *Brahma*-nature is a spiritual disposition uninfluenced by the cravings of the flesh, and forming a sort of cleared ground for the germination of *bhakti* or true devotion to God.

55. By devotion, etc., the devotee realizes God as the lover of every creature, etc., (*vide* V. 29), and then finds a home in His bosom. The expression *tadanantaram* is variously explained, *viz*.

(1) immediately, forthwith or then.

(2) *That* the inseparate (with Me, the Personal God) *i.e.* the Supreme Brahma (*That* being often used for the Supreme Brahma), *vide* VIII. 3 and XIV. 27.

(3) That the inseparate with Me, *viz.* *My Superior Nature* (VII. 5) which is a part of Me.

56. resigned to Me, etc., pious resignation in *all efforts* of active life is not inferior in efficacy to the

Understanding, *Buddhi,* reason, conscience, judgment (vide *Faculties*). II. 41, 44, 49-53, 63, 65, 66; III. 4, 26, 40, 42, 43; IV. 18; V. 11, 17, 28; VI. 9, 21, 25, 43; VII. 4, 10, 24; VIII. 7; X. 4, 10; XII. 4, 8, 14; XIII. 5; XV. 20; XVI. 9; XVIII. 17, 29-32, 37, 49, 51, 57.

Yoga, literally, union or communion: used to signify *union* with *right activity,* or with *right thinking,* or with *right feel-*

ing, or with *right faith;* and to indicate the correlative idea of *Sannyasa* which is the *avoidance* or *rejection* of *wrong activity, wrong thinking, wrong feeling or wrong faith.* II. 39, 48-50, 53; III. 3, 7; IV. 1-3, 27, 28, 38, 41, 42; V. 1, 2, 4, 5, 6, 7, 21; VI. 2-4, 12, 16, 17, 18, 19, 20, 23, 29, 33, 36, 37, 41, 44-47; VII. 1; VIII. 8, 10, 12, 27, 28; IX. 22, 28; X. 7, 10; XI. 47; XII. 1, 6; XIII. 10, 24; XIV. 26; XVI. 1; XVIII. 33, 52, 57, 75, 78.